Knowledge and Reasoning for Language Processing 2006

(KRAQ 06)

Held at EACL 2006

Trento, Italy
3 April 2006

ISBN: 978-1-61738-486-8

Printed from e-media with permission by:

Curran Associates, Inc.
57 Morehouse Lane
Red Hook, NY 12571
www.proceedings.com

Some format issues inherent in the e-media version may also appear in this print version.

Printed by Curran Associates, Inc. (2010)

Association for Computational Linguistics
209 N. Eighth Street
Stroudsburg, Pennsylvania 18360

Phone: 1-570-476-8006
Fax: 1-570-476-0860

acl@aclweb.org

Contents and Schedule

Preface

Recent foundational, methodological and technological developments in advanced language processing resources and techniques, knowledge representation, advanced reasoning forms not necessarily based on unification, applied pragmatics, and recent progress in HLT make it possible to foresee the elaboration of much more accurate, cooperative and robust systems dedicated to NLP in general and to answering questions in particular. The development of more robust evaluation techniques make it also possible to identify results, weaknesses and future directions.

The goal of this workshop is to enhance cooperation between participants with an AI background and the NLP community. After the 2005 edition, associated with IJCAI in Edinburgh, the 2006 version of this workshop is organized around major questions of interest to a number of NLP, AI, HLT and pragmatics people. Besides Question-Answering, which is a hot topic in this perspective, the workshop addresses areas of NLP that require knowledge and reasoning to perform better.
The following topics and the main points addressed during the workshop:

- Reasoning aspects: dedicated inference schemas (in semantics, in pragmatics and in interpretation phases), intelligent information processing, resolving redundancies or inconsistencies, e.g. via fusion in NLG, search criteria expansion models (e.g. relaxation techniques) in QA, inference in summarization, and reasoning under uncertainty or with incomplete knowledge, e.g. in dialogue.
- Knowledge representation and integration: levels of knowledge involved in NLP (e.g. ontologies, domain knowledge), and their relations to language, knowledge extraction models and techniques, and coherence and integration.
- Flexible and interactive systems possibly including a user model,
- Language processing: question processing, language generation (e.g. lexical choice, planning), use of language resources to develop reasoning schemas (e.g. lexical semantics relations), reasoning to resolve ambiguities or references, explanation production (showing sources and inferences, reporting data incompleteness, etc.), argumentation, and intelligent language tutoring systems.

Farah Benamara and Patrick Saint-Dizier, co-organizers

KRAQ'06:
Knowledge and Reasoning for Language Processing

Workshop Organizers:
Farah Benamara and Patrick Saint Dizier, IRIT, France

Programme Committee
Farah Benamara, IRIT, France
Johan Bos, University of Edinburgh, UK
Eduard Hovy, ISI, USA
Daniel Kayser, LIPN, France
Asanee Kawtrakul, Kasererart univ. Thailand
Mark Maybury, The MITRE Corp., USA
Yuji Matsumoto, Nara, Japan
Marie-Francine Moens, KUL, Belgium
John Prager, IBM, USA
Bali Ranaivo, Univ. Sains Malaysia, Malaysia
Ehud Reiter, University of Aberdeen, UK
Patrick Saint Dizier, IRIT, CNRS, France
Sudeshna Sarkar, IIT Kharagpur, India
Mathiew Stone, Center of Cognitive Science, Rutgers, USA

Invited speakers
Farah Benamara, IRIT, France
Gosse Bouma, Information Science Rijksuniversiteit Groningen, NL.
Dominique Laurent: Synapse, France.

The conference, the workshop and the tutorials are sponsored by:

Center for the Evaluation of Language and Communication Technologies

Celct
c/o BIC, Via dei Solteri, 38
38100 Trento, Italy
http://www.celct.it

XEROX®
Research Centre Europe

Xerox Research Centre Europe
6 Chemin de Maupertuis
38240 Meylan, France
http://www.xrce.xerox.com

CELI s.r.l.
Corso Moncalieri, 21
10131 Torino, Italy
http://www.celi.it

THALES

Thales
45 rue de Villiers
92526 Neuilly-sur-Seine Cedex, France
http://www.thalesgroup.com

EACL-2006 is supported by

Trentino S.p.a. and Metalsistem Group

Language and Reasoning for Question Answering: State of the Art and Future Directions

Farah Benamara
Institut de Recherche en Informatique de Toulouse
118, route de Narbonne, 31062 Toulouse, France
benamara@irit.fr

Abstract

The research community states that QA systems should support the integration of deeper modes of language understanding as well as more elaborated reasoning schemas in order to boost the performances of current QA systems as well as the quality and the relevance of the produced answers.

Depending on the complexity of the question and the associated passages, more or less complex strategies can be used, such as :

- deep semantic analysis of NL questions such as anaphora resolutions,
- context and ambiguity detection,
- responses to unanticipated questions or to resolve situations in which no answer is found in the data sources,
- models for answer completeness,
- dialogue and interactive QA scenario,
- models for answer fusion from different sources, etc.

We focus in this talk on the role of reasoning in a QA process by answering the following questions: what kind of reasoning capabilities can be used ? on what kind of resources can they be built on ? at what extend they can be used when developing realistic systems ?

Based on the synthesis of the current state of the art, the second part of the talk describes a general typology of inference at different levels: deep semantic analysis of both NL questions and passages, textual entailment, pragmatic inference and context detection, etc. The related formalisms as well as a description of some current QA systems based on these techniques are also presented.

Linguistic Knowledge and Question Answering

Gosse Bouma
Information Science
Groningen University
•g.bouma•@rug.nl

Abstract

The availability of robust and deep syntactic parsing can improve the performance of Question Answering systems. This is illustrated using examples from Joost, a Dutch QA system which has been used for both open (CLEF) and closed domain QA.

1 Linguistically Informed IR

Information retrieval is used in most QA systems to filter out relevant passages from large document collections to narrow down the search for answer extraction modules in a QA system. Given a full syntactic analysis of the text collection, it becomes feasible to exploit linguistic information as a knowledge source for IR. Using Apache's IR system Lucene, we can index the document collection along various linguistic dimensions, such as part of speech tags, named entity classes, and dependency relations. Tiedemann (2005) uses a genetic algorithm to optimize the use of such an extended IR index, and shows that it leads to significant improvements of IR performance.

2 Acquisition of Lexical Knowledge

Syntactic similarity measures can be used for automatic acquisition of lexical knowledge required for QA, as well as for answer extraction and ranking. For instance, in van der Plas and Bouma (2005) it is shown that automatically acquired class-labels for named entities improve the accuracy of answering general WH-questions (i.e. *Which ferry sank in the Baltic Sea?*) and questions which ask for the definition of a named entity (i.e. *Who is Nelson Mandela?* or *What is MTV?*).

3 Off-line answer extraction

Off-line extraction of answers to frequent question types can be based on dependency patterns and coreference resolution (Bouma et al., 2005; Mur and van der Plas, 2006), leading to higher recall (compared to systems using surface patterns). Closed-domain (medical) QA can benefit from the fact that dependency relations allow answers to be identified for questions which are not restricted to specific named entity classes, i.e. definitions, causes, symptoms, etc. Answering definition questions, for instance, is a task which has motivated approaches that go well beyond the techniques used for answering factoid questions. In Fahmi and Bouma (2006) it is shown that syntactic patterns can be used to extract potential definition sentences from Wikipedia, and that syntactic features of these sentences (in combination with obvious clues such as the position of the sentence in the document) can be used to improve the accuracy of an automatic classifier which distinguishes definitions from non-definitions in the extracted data set.

4 Joost

Joost is a QA system for Dutch which incorporates the features mentioned above, using the Alpino parser for Dutch to parse (offline) the document collections as well as (interactively) user questions. It has been used for the open-domain monolingual QA task of CLEF 2005, as well as for closed domain medical QA. For CLEF, the full Dutch text collection (4 years of newspaper text, approximately 80 million words) has been parsed. For the medical QA system, we have been using a mixture of texts from general and medical encyclopedia, medical reference works, and web pages dedicated to medical topics. The medical data are from mixed sources and contain a fair amount of domain specific terminology. Although the Alpino system is robust enough to deal with such material, we believe that the accuracy of linguistic analysis on this task can be further improved by incorporating domain specific terminological resources. We are currently investigating methods for acquiring such knowledge automatically from the encyclopedia sources.

References

Gosse Bouma, Jori Mur, and Gertjan van Noord. 2005. Reasoning over dependency relations for QA. In *Proceedings of the IJCAI workshop on Knowledge and Reasoning for Answering Questions (KRAQ)*, pages 15–21, Edinburgh.

Ismail Fahmi and Gosse Bouma. 2006. Learning to identify definitions using syntactic features. In Roberto Basili and Alessandro Moschitti, editors, *Proceedings of the EACL workshop on Learning Structured Information in Natural Language Applications*, Trento, Italy.

Jori Mur and Lonneke van der Plas. 2006. Anaphora resolution for off-line answer extraction using instances. submitted.

Jörg Tiedemann. 2005. Integrating linguistic knowledge in passage retrieval for question answering. In *Proceedings of EMNLP 2005*, pages 939–946, Vancouver.

Lonneke van der Plas and Gosse Bouma. 2005. Automatic acquisition of lexico-semantic knowledge for question answering. In *Proceedings of Ontolex 2005 – Ontologies and Lexical Resources*, Jeju Island, South Korea.

Interpretation and Generation in a Knowledge-Based Tutorial System

Myroslava O. Dzikovska, Charles B. Callaway, Elaine Farrow
Human Communication Research Centre, University of Edinburgh
2 Buccleuch Place, Edinburgh, EH8 9LW,
United Kingdom,
{mdzikovs,ccallawa,efarrow}@inf.ed.ac.uk

Abstract

We discuss how deep interpretation and generation can be integrated with a knowledge representation designed for question answering to build a tutorial dialogue system. We use a knowledge representation known to perform well in answering exam-type questions and show that to support tutorial dialogue it needs additional features, in particular, compositional representations for interpretation and structured explanation representations.

1 Introduction

Human tutoring is known to help students learn compared with reading textbooks, producing up to two standard deviations in learning gain (Bloom, 1984). Tutorial systems, in particular cognitive tutors which model the inner state of a student's knowledge, help learning but result in only up to 1 standard deviation learning gain (Anderson et al., 1995). One current research hypothesis is that this difference is accounted for by interactive dialogue, which allows students to ask questions freely, and tutors to adapt their direct feedback and presentation style to the individual student's needs.

Adding natural language dialogue to a tutorial system is a complex task. Many existing tutorial dialogue systems rely on pre-authored curriculum scripts (Person et al., 2000) or finite-state machines (Rosé et al., 2001) without detailed knowledge representations. These systems are easy to design for curriculum providers, but offer limited flexibility because the writer has to predict all possible student questions and answers.

We argue that the ability to interpret novel, context-dependent student questions and answers, and offer tailored feedback and explanations is important in tutorial dialogue, and that a domain knowledge representation and reasoning engine is necessary to support these applications. We discuss our knowledge representation, and the issues of integrating it with state-of-the-art interpretation and generation components to build a knowledge-based tutorial dialogue system.

Our application domain is in basic electricity and electronics, specifically teaching a student how to predict the behavior and interpret measurements in series and parallel circuits. This is a conceptual domain - that is, students are primarily focused on learning concepts such as voltage and current, and their relationships with the real world. The students use a circuit simulator to build circuits, and their questions and answers depend on the current context.

There are various sources of context-dependency in our domain. Students and tutors refer to specific items in the simulation (*e.g.*, "Which lightbulbs will be lit in these circuits?"), and may phrase their answers in an unexpected way, for example, by saying "the lightbulbs in 2 and 4 will be out" instead of naming the lit lightbulbs. Moreover, students may build arbitrary circuits not included in the question, either because they make mistakes, or because a tutor instructs them to do so as part of remediation. Thus it would be difficult to produce and maintain a finite-state machine to predict all possible situations, both for interpreting the input and for generating feedback based on the state of the environment and the previous dialogue context: a domain reasoner is necessary to handle such unanticipated situations correctly.

We describe a tutorial system which uses a description logic-based knowledge representation to generate intelligent explanations and answers to a student's questions, as well as to interpret the student's language at all stages of the dialogue. Our approach relies on using an existing wide-coverage parser for domain-independent syntactic parsing and semantic interpretation, as well as a wide-coverage deep generation system. We discuss the issues which arise in connecting such resources to a domain knowledge representation in a practical system.

2 Motivation

A good teaching method for basic electricity and electronics is eliciting cognitive dissonance (Schaffer and McDermott, 1992; Arnold and Millar, 1987) which we are implementing as a "predict-verify-evaluate" (PVE) cycle. The students are asked to make predictions about the behavior of a schematic circuit and then build it in a simulation environment. If the observed results do not match their predictions, a discussion ensues, where the computer tutor helps a student learn the relevant concepts. The PVE exercises are complemented with exercises asking the students to identify properties of circuits in diagrams and to interpret a circuit's behavior.

Thus, the system has to answer questions about circuits which students build and manipulate dynamically in a simulation environment, and produce explanations and feedback tailored to that individual context. This relies on the following system capabilities:

- *Understanding and giving explanations.* Since the system relies on inducing cognitive dissonance, it should be able to explain to the student why their prediction for a specific circuit was incorrect, and also verify explanations given by a student.

- *Unrestricted language input with reference resolution.* Similar to other conceptual domains (VanLehn et al., 2002) the language observed in corpus studies is varied and syntactically complex. Additionally, in our domain students refer to items on screen, e.g. "the lightbulb in 5", which requires the system to make the connection between the language descriptions and the actual objects in the environment.

- *Tailored generation.* The level of detail in the explanations offered should be sensitive to student knowledge of the domain. Tutorial utterances should be natural and use correct terminology even if a student doesn't.

To support answering questions and giving explanations, we chose the KM knowledge representation environment (Clark and Porter, 1999) as a basis for our implementation. KM is a description-logic based language which has been used to represent facts and rules in a HALO system for AP chemistry tests (Barker et al., 2004). It supports the generation of explanations and obtained the highest explanation scores in an independent evaluation based on an AP chemistry exam (Friedland et al., 2004). Thus it is a good choice to provide reasoning support for explanations and answering novel questions in a tutorial system. However, KM has not been used previously in connection with natural language input for question answering, and we discuss how the limitations of KM representations affect the interpretation process in Section 4.

We use a deep domain-independent parser and grammar to support language interpretation, and a deep generator to provide natural sounding and context-dependent text. Both deep parsing and generation provide the context adaptivity we need, but they are time-consuming to build for a specific domain. Now that a number of deep domain-independent parsing and generation systems are available in the community, our research goal is to investigate the issues in integrating them with the knowledge representation for question answering to support the requirements of a tutorial dialogue system. We focus on context-dependent explanation understanding and generation as a primary tutoring task in our domain. Section 3 discusses our representations, Section 4 presents the issues arising in knowledge representation to support interpretation, and Section 5 discusses the requirements for appropriate explanation generation and how it can be integrated into the system.

3 Representations

From the point of view of tutoring, the most important requirement on the knowledge representation is that system reasoning should closely match human reasoning, so that it can be explained to students in meaningful terms. Thus, for example, a numerical circuit simulator is well suited for dynamically displaying circuit behaviors, but not for conceptually tutoring basic circuits, because it hides physics principles behind complex mathematical equations that are not suitable for learners.

To design our knowledge representation we started with a set of lessons for our domain designed by psychologists experienced in designing training courses for physics and simulated environments. The lessons were used in a data collection environment with experienced tutors conducting tutoring sessions over a text chat interface. Each student and tutor were required to go through the materials presented as a set of slides and solve pre-defined exercises, but the students asked questions to get help with problem-solving. The tutor had complete freedom to choose how to answer student questions and how to remediate when students made mistakes. We are using this data set to study the types of errors that students make as well as the language used by both students and tutors. The latter serves as a guide to developing our interpretation and generation components.

In addition to the set of materials, the course designers provided a "glossary" of concepts and facts that students need to learn and use in explanations, containing approximately 200 concepts and rules in a form which should be used in model explanations. We then developed our knowledge representation so that concepts listed in the glossary were represented as KM concepts, and facts are represented as rules for computing slots.

An example KM representation for our domain is shown in Figure 1. It represents the fact that a lightbulb will be on if it is in a complete path (i.e. a closed path containing a battery). The explanation is generated using the comment structure *[lightbulbstate]* shown in Figure 2 (slightly simplified for readability). Explanations are generated separately from reasoning in the KM system because reasoning in general contains too many low-level details. For example, our rule for computing a lightbulb state includes two facts: that the lightbulb has to be in a complete path with a battery, and that a lightbulb is always in one state only (i.e. it cannot be broken and on at the same time). The latter is required for proof completeness, but is too trivial to be mentioned to students. KM therefore requires knowledge engineers to explicitly designate the facts to be used in explanations.

This representation allows KM to generate detailed explanations by using a template string and then explaining the supporting facts. An example of a full explanation, together with the adjustments needed to use it in dialogue rather than as a complete answer, is given in Section 5.

Currently, KM only supports generating explanations, but not verifying them. The explanation mechanism produces explanations as text directly from the knowledge representation, as shown in Figure 2(a). This generation method is not well suited for a tutorial dialogue system, because it does not take context into account, as discussed in Section 5. Therefore, we are designing a structured representation for explanations to be produced by the KM explanation mechanism instead of using English sentences, shown in Figure 2(b). This will allow us to generate more flexible explanations (Section 5) and also to interpret student explanations (Section 4).

4 Interpretation

The interpretation process consists of parsing, reference resolution, dialogue act recognition and diagnosing student answers. We discuss reference resolution and diagnosis here as these are the two steps impacted by the knowledge representation issues. As a basic example we will use the student answer from the following pair:[1]

Problem: For each circuit, which lightbulbs will be lit? Explain.

Student: the bulbs in 1 and 3 are lit because they are in a closed path with a battery

To respond to this answer properly, the system must complete at least the following tasks. First, it must resolve "the bulbs in 1 and 3" to corresponding object IDs in the knowledge base, for example, *LB-13-1-1* and *LB-13-3-1*. Then, it must verify that the student statement is factually correct. This includes verifying that the lightbulbs in 1 and 3 will be lit, and that each of them is in a closed path with a battery. Finally, it must verify that the student explanation is correct. This is separate from verifying factual correctness. For example, a statement "because they are in a closed path" is true for both of those lightbulbs, but it is not a complete explanation, because a lightbulb may be in a closed path which does not contain a battery, where it won't be lit.

[1]These utterances come from our corpus, though most of the student answers are not as easy to parse. We are working on robust parsing methods to address the issues in parsing less coherent utterances.

```
(every LightBulb has
  (state ((must-be-a Electrical-Usage-State) (exactly 1 Electrical-Usage-State)
        (if (the is-damaged of Self) then *Broken-Usage-State
           else (if (has-value (oneof ?batt in (the powered-by of Self)))
                                      where ((the state of ?batt) = *Charged-Power-State)))
                then *On-Usage-State else *Off-Usage-State) [lightbulbstate])))
```

Figure 1: The representation of a lightbulb in our KM database

```
(a)(comment [lightbulbstate]
     (:sentence ("a working lightbulb is on if it is in a complete path with a charged battery"))
     (:supporting-facts (:triple Self powered-by *) (forall (the powered-by of Self) (:triple It state *)))
(b)(comment [lightbulbstate]
     (:rule :object LightBulb :fact (?lb state *On-Usage-State)
        :requires ((?lb powered-by ?v1) (?v1 instance-of Battery) (?v1 state *Charged-Power-State))
        :bindings ((?lb ⟨ Self ⟩) (?v1 ⟨ the powered-by of Self ⟩)) )
```

Figure 2: A sample comment structure to generate an explanation for a lit lightbulb (a) The KM text template (b) a new structured representation. Items in angle brackets are computed dynamically

4.1 Interpreting Factual Statements

We use the TRIPS dialogue parser (Dzikovska, 2004) for interpretation. The TRIPS parser provides a two-layer architecture where the utterance meaning is represented using a domain-independent semantic ontology and syntax. The domain-independent representation is used for discourse processing tasks such as reference resolution, but it is connected to the domain-specific knowledge representation by mapping between the domain-independent and domain-specific ontologies (Dzikovska et al., 2003; Dzikovska, 2004). This architecture allows us to separate linguistic and domain-specific knowledge and easily specialize to new domains.

When applied in our domain, the TRIPS interpretation architecture was helpful in getting the interpretation started quickly, because we only needed to extend the lexicon with specific terms related to basic electricity and electronics (*e.g.*, "multimeter"), while other lexical items and syntactic constructions were provided in the domain-independent part.

The reference resolution module operates on TRIPS domain-independent representations sending queries to KM as necessary, because the TRIPS representations offer linguistic features to guide reference resolution not available in the representations used for reasoning. We use a recursive reference resolution algorithm similar to Byron (2002) which first resolves "1 and 3" are resolved as names for *Circuit-13-1* and *Circuit-13-3*,[2] and then queries KM to find all lightbulbs in those circuits. Dialogue context is used to interpret the reference resolution results. In this case, the context does not matter because the question sets up all lightbulbs on screen as contextually relevant. But if the student had said "the ones in 1 and 3", the query would be for all components in circuits 1 and 3, and then our algorithm will filter the query results based on the question context to retain only lightbulbs.

Once the references are resolved, the whole sentence is converted to a KM statement which represents the student utterance, in our case *(the state of LB13-1-1) = *On-Usage-State*, where *LB13-1-1* is the lightbulb obtained by reference resolution. This statement is sent to the KM system, which verifies that it is correct. This procedure allows us to use dialogue context in understanding, and also to check correctness of answers easily, even if they are phrased in an unanticipated way.

However, even with the layer of separation of linguistic and domain knowledge provided by the TRIPS architecture, we found that the need to support interpretation in a compositional way influences the interaction with knowledge representation. There are many ways to express the same query to KM, which differ in efficiency. Two ex-

[2] This step is not trivial, because on other slides the label "1" refers to terminals or other components rather than whole circuits, and therefore there is no 1-to-1 correspondence between names and objects in the environment.

(a) (allof ?x in (the all-instances of LightBulb) where ((the components of Circuit-13-1) include ?x))
(allof ?x (LightBulb ?x) and (components Circuit-13-1 ?x))
(b) (allof ?comp in (the components of Circuit-13-1) where (?comp isa LightBulb))
(allof ?x (components Circuit-13-1 ?x) and (LightBulb ?x))

Figure 3: KM Queries to to retrieve all lightbulbs in a circuit with corresponding first-order logic glosses.

ample queries to ask the same question are given in Figure 3. While their first order logic semantics is equivalent except for the order of conjuncts, they are expressed in a very different way in the KM syntax. Version (b) is more efficient to ask, because it retrieves the components of circuit 1 first, a smaller set than the set of all lightbulbs.

This asymmetry presents a challenge to both language interpretation and knowledge engineering. Existing reference resolution algorithms (Byron, 2002; Bos, 2004) expect the queries for "the lightbulb" and "the lightbulb in 1" to be strictly compositional in the sense that the phrase "the lightbulb" will be represented identically in both cases, and "in 1" is represented as an additional constraint on the lightbulbs. This corresponds to the query variant (a) in the system. Otherwise a large amount of query-specific transformations may be required to produce queries for complex noun phrase descriptions, diminishing the scalability of the approach.

We had to spend a significant portion of time in the project developing an efficient and compositional knowledge representation. Our current solution is to prefer compositionality over efficiency, even though it impacts performance in some cases, but we are working on a more general solution. Instead of converting directly to KM from domain-independent language representations, we will convert all queries in a FOL-like syntax shown in Figure 3 which uses concepts from the KM representation, but where all conjuncts are treated identically in the syntax. The problem of converting this representation to the optimal KM form can then be seen as an instance of query optimization. For example, we can reorder the conjuncts putting the relations which include an instance constant (*e.g.*, (the components of Circuit-13-1)) first in the query, because they are more likely to limit the search to small sets of objects. This representation can be easily converted in the KM syntax, and is also useful for explanation understanding and generation as discussed below.

4.2 Explanation Understanding

While KM has facilities for generating explanations, it does not have support for reading in a student explanation and verifying it. We devised a method to support this functionality with the aid of KM explanation generation mechanism. Any time a student offers an explanation, the KM reasoner will be called to generate its own explanation for the same fact, in the structured format shown in Figure 2(b). Then the student explanation (converted into the same intermediate syntax) can be matched against the KM-generated explanation to verify that it is complete, or else that certain parts are missing.

In our example, the student explanation "because they are in a closed path with a battery" will be represented as *(?pa instance-of Path) (?pa is-closed t) (?b instance-of Battery) (?pa contains ?b) (?pa contains LB-13-1-1).*[3] This explanation does not directly match into the explanation structure from Figure 2(b), because it uses the more specific term "in closed path with a battery" rather than the more general term "in complete path" (represented by the *powered-by* slot). However, as part of generating the explanation, an explanation structure for the *powered-by* will be generated, and it will include the facts *(?pa is-closed t) (?pa contains ?b).* This will match the student explanation. It will be up to the tutorial module to decide whether to accept the explanation "as is", or lead the student to use the more precise terminology, as discussed in Section 5.

This method can address student explanations as long as they correspond to parts of typical explanations, and identify missing parts. The biggest open problem we face is equivalent inferences. For example, a student may say "A lightbulb is not on" instead of "a lightbulb is off". KM reasoning handles those differences when verifying factual correctness, but KM does not support similar reasoning for matching explanations (which

[3]Here "they" would be resolved first to a set of lightbulbs, and each instance will be treated separately to verify that the explanation applies.

would correspond to verifying full proofs rather than individual facts). We are considering bringing a theorem prover to reason over intermediate representations together with KM axioms to help interpret explanations, as done in (Makatchev et al., 2004; Bos, 2005).

5 Generation

The task of the utterance generation component is to produce tutorial dialogue, such as asking new questions of the student, conveying the correctness of their answers, and giving explanations. Explanations may be given in response to a student's direct 'why' question or when a student has erred and the pedagogical reasoner has decided that an explanation is the best remediation strategy. In each case, the utterance generator must not only provide a correct, thorough and coherent explanation, but must tailor it so that the student doesn't receive too much or too little information. To be tailorable, explanations must be derived from the represented domain knowledge and from what the tutoring system knows about the student (e.g., their recent performance).

Directly producing explanations by appending together pieces of hand-written strings as in Figure 2(a) usually results in long explanations that contain little detail of interest to the student. Figure 4 contains one such example explanation generated by the KM system in our domain and derived from a query based on the production rule in Figure 1. This explanation makes sense in answering an exam question, as intended in the KM system, but it is not necessarily helpful in dialogue.

As an example, suppose the student had incorrectly answered the question in Section 4, and the tutoring system decides to correctly explain why the lightbulbs are lit. Usually, a full explanation is not necessary in these cases. In the case where a student gave an incomplete explanation, namely leaving out the necessary mention of the battery, a simple response of the form "Yes, but don't forget the battery" will be infinitely more helpful than the full explanation. If the student's explanation is completely correct, but they have failed to notice a change in the environment, the more appropriate explanation is "The lightbulb is in a closed path, as well as the battery, but the battery is not operational". Furthermore, if a student has shown that they are knowledgeable about certain fundamental facts, such as what states a lightbulb may be in, statements like "A lightbulb can be on, off or broken" should be removed.

Adding this reasoning directly to the knowledge base would make it unwieldy and unmodifiable, and the string-based generation in KM comments does not allow for adapting explanations based on external knowledge such as a student model. To adapt the KM explanation mechanism to support such context-dependent generation, instead of creating explanations via template strings, we have devised the representation presented in Figure 2(b) that is based on semantics and allows us to modify an explanation after it has been produced by the KM reasoning process but before it has been converted into a string representation.

Based on this semantic representation, explanation content can be selected more appropriately. If the interpreter discussed in Section 4.2 determines that parts of the explanation from the *:requires* field are missing, the generation can focus only on that part of the explanation. The requirements list would also be used to determine if the student is not aware of environment properties, such as that a battery is damaged. Finally, the facts known to the student can be removed if the corresponding semantic forms were used in previous explanations.

In addition to selecting the explanation content properly, it is important that the responses given to the student sound fluid and are easy to understand. In dialogue, in particular, it is important that pronouns can be generated based on references important for the student, and avoid repetitiveness in syntax. Knowledge of linguistic features such as number and gender, and also knowledge of what was previously mentioned in the discourse, is necessary to support such natural text generation.

Deep generation utilizes this represented knowledge along with grammatical and lexical knowledge of a language, rather than hand-written strings, to produce utterances. Our current implementation uses a custom utterance generation component and the STORYBOOK (Callaway and Lester, 2002) deep text generator modified to work in a dialogue context. Once the explanation content is selected, it is passed to the STORYBOOK system to produce the actual utterance text.

6 Discussion and Related Work

Existing tutorial dialogue systems most often rely on one of two approaches for interpretation: they either use wide coverage but shallow language

```
A lightbulb can be on, off or broken.
A working lightbulb is on if it is in a complete path with a charged battery.
  The complete paths of a component are those which are valid, closed, and complete.
    A path is complete if it is a closed path with at least one battery and at least...
      A path is closed if it is a valid path, a sequence of more than two terminals, ...
        A path is valid if it is a single sequence with more than one terminal, all ...
        The path (:seq t1-13-1-3 t1-13-1-2 t1-13-1-1 t1-13-1-4) is valid.
      The path (:seq t1-13-1-3 t1-13-1-2 t1-13-1-1 t1-13-1-4) is closed.
        ... 6 lines showing that the path contains both L1-13-1-1 and B1-13-1-1 ...
    The path (:seq t1-13-1-3 t1-13-1-2 t1-13-1-1 t1-13-1-4) is complete.
  L1-13-1-1 is in a complete path with B1-13-1-1.
  A battery is charged unless it is damaged.
  B1-13-1-1 is charged.
L1-13-1-1 is on.
```

Figure 4: Untailored text produced by appending strings from production rules.

interpretation techniques (e.g. LSA (Person et al., 2000), finite-state parsing (Glass, 2001)) in combination with shallow knowledge representations (tutorial scripts or FSA-based knowledge construction dialogues), or they use deep KR&R systems but with highly domain-specific parsing and semantic interpretation (e.g. ATLAS-ANDES (Rosé et al., 2001), PACT (Aleven et al., 2002)).

The Why2-Atlas system (VanLehn et al., 2002) makes progress on combining wide coverage interpretation with deep knowledge representation by utilizing a wide-coverage syntactic grammar (Rosé, 2000) and a theorem prover to interpret student essays (Makatchev et al., 2004). However, once the misconceptions are diagnosed, the remediation is done via KCDs, with very limited language input and pre-authored responses, and without allowing students to ask questions. Our approach attempts to address issues which arise in making remediation more flexible and dependent on context, while still relying on wide-coverage language interpretation and generation.

The issues we encountered in integrating compositional interpretation and reference resolution with efficient knowledge representation is similar to a known problem in natural language interfaces to databases which may contain slots with complex meanings. (Stallard, 1986) solves this problem by providing inference schemas linking complex-valued slots with compositional representations. Our solution in mapping domain-independent to domain-specific representation is similar, but stricter compositionality is needed for reference resolution support, placing additional constraints on knowledge engineering as we discussed in Section 4.

We glossed over the interpretation issues related to metonymy and other imprecise formulations in questions (Aleven et al., 2002). A taxonomy of imprecise manual question encodings by domain experts is presented in (Fan and Porter, 2004). They also propose an algorithm to address loosely encoded questions using ontological knowledge. This algorithm in effect performs question interpretation, and we are planning to incorporate it into our interpretation mechanism to help interpret question representations obtained automatically during language interpretation.

Text generation of the type that can handle the necessary linguistic phenomena needed have not been implemented in tutoring systems that use dialogue. The DIAG-NLP tutorial dialogue system (Eugenio et al., 2005) shows that structured explanations from deep generation supported by knowledge representation and reasoning improve learning. However, it does not engage in a dialogue with the user, and in this paper we showed that explanations need to be further adjusted in dialogue based on previous student responses and knowledge. Deep generation using context has been used in some other types of dialogue systems such as collaborative problem solving (Stent, 2001), and we expect that the approaches used in content selection and planning in those systems will also transfer to our deep generation system.

7 Conclusions

We discussed the implementation of a tutorial dialogue system which relies on a domain knowledge representation to verify student answers and offer appropriate explanations. Integration with domain-independent interpretation and generation components places additional requirements on knowledge representation, and we showed how an existing knowledge representation mechanisms used in answering exam questions can be adapted to the more complex task of tutoring, including interpreting student explanations and generating appropriate feedback.

Acknowledgments

This material is based upon work supported by a grant from The Office of Naval Research number N000149910165.

References

V. Aleven, O. Popescu, and K. Koedinger. 2002. Pilot-testing a tutorial dialogue system that supports self-explanation. *Lecture Notes in Computer Science*, 2363.

J. R. Anderson, A. T. Corbett, K. R. Koedinger, and R. Pelletier. 1995. Cognitive tutors: Lessons learned. *The Journal of the Learning Sciences*, 4(2):167–207.

M. Arnold and R. Millar. 1987. Being constructive: An alternative approach to the teaching of introductory ideas in electricity. *International Journal of Science Education*, 9:553–563.

K. Barker, V. K. Chaudhri, S. Y. Chaw, P. Clark, J. Fan, D. Israel, S. Mishra, B. W. Porter, P. Romero, D. Tecuci, and P. Z. Yeh. 2004. A question-answering system for AP chemistry: Assessing KR&R technologies. In *KR*, pages 488–497.

B. S. Bloom. 1984. The two sigma problem: The search for methods of group instruction as effective as one-to-one tutoring. *Educational Researcher*, 13:3–16.

Johan Bos. 2004. Computational semantics in discourse: Underspecification, resolution, and inference. *Journal of Logic, Language and Information*, 13(2):139–157.

Johan Bos. 2005. Towards wide-coverage semantic interpretation. In *Proceedings of Sixth International Workshop on Computational Semantics (IWCS-6)*.

Donna K. Byron. 2002. *Resolving Pronominal Reference to Abstract Entities*. Ph.D. thesis, University of Rochester.

Charles B. Callaway and James C. Lester. 2002. Narrative prose generation. *Artificial Intelligence*, 139(2):213–252, August.

P. Clark and B. Porter, 1999. *KM (1.4): Users Manual*. http://www.cs.utexas.edu/users/mfkb/km.

M. O. Dzikovska, M. D. Swift, and J. F. Allen. 2003. Integrating linguistic and domain knowledge for spoken dialogue systems in multiple domains. In *Proceedings of IJCAI-03 Workshop on Knowledge and Reasoning in Practical Dialogue Systems*.

M. O. Dzikovska. 2004. *A Practical Semantic Representation For Natural Language Parsing*. Ph.D. thesis, University of Rochester.

B. Di Eugenio, D. Fossati, D. Yu, S. Haller, and M. Glass. 2005. Natural language generation for intelligent tutoring systems: A case study. In *12th International Conference on Artificial Intelligence in Education*, pages 217–224.

J. Fan and B. W. Porter. 2004. Interpreting loosely encoded questions. In *Proceedings of the Nineteenth National Conference on Artificial Intelligence, Sixteenth Conference on Innovative Applications of Artificial Intelligence*, pages 399–405.

N. S. Friedland, P. G. Allen, M. J. Witbrock, G. Matthews, N. Salay, P. Miraglia, J. Angele, S. Staab, D. Israel, V. K. Chaudhri, B. W. Porter, K. Barker, and P. Clark. 2004. Towards a quantitative, platform-independent analysis of knowledge systems. In *KR*, pages 507–515.

M. Glass. 2001. Processing language input in the CIRCSIM-tutor intelligent tutoring system. In J. Moore, C. L. Redfield, and W. L. Johnson, editors, *Artificial Intelligence in Education*. IOS press.

M. Makatchev, P. W. Jordan, and K. VanLehn. 2004. Abductive theorem proving for analyzing student explanations to guide feedback in intelligent tutoring systems. *J. Autom. Reasoning*, 32(3):187–226.

N. Person, A.C. Graesser, D. Harter, and E. Mathews. 2000. Dialog move generation and conversation management in autotutor. In *Workshop Notes of the AAAI '00 Fall Symposium on Building Dialogue Systems for Tutorial Applications*.

C. Rosé, P. Jordan, M. Ringenberg, S. Siler, K. VanLehn, and A. Weinstein. 2001. Interactive conceptual tutoring in atlas-andes. In *Proceedings of AI in Education 2001 Conference*.

C. Rosé. 2000. A framework for robust semantic interpretation. In *Proceedings 1st Meeting of the North American Chapter of the Association for Computational Linguistics*.

P. S. Schaffer and L. C. McDermott. 1992. Research as a guide for curriculum development: An example from introductory electricity. part ii: Design of instructional strategies. *American Journal of Physics*, 60(11):1003–1013.

D. G. Stallard. 1986. A terminological simplification transformation for natural language question-answering systems. In *ACL Proceedings, 24th Annual Meeting*, pages 241–246.

A. Stent. 2001. *Dialogue Systems as Conversational Partners: Applying conversation acts theory to natural language generation for task-oriented mixed-initiative spoken dialogue*. Ph.D. thesis, University of Rochester, Rochester, NY, August.

K. VanLehn, P. Jordan, C. P. Rosé, and The Natural Language Tutoring Group. 2002. The architecture of why2-atlas: a coach for qualitative physics essay writing. In *Proceedings of Intelligent Tutoring Systems Conference*.

Using Application-Specific Ontologies to Improve Performance in a Bottom-up Parser

Marta Gatius **Meritxell González**
TALP Research Center
Technical University of Catalonia
Barcelona, Spain
{gatius,mgonzalez}@lsi.upc.edu

Abstract

This paper describes how the application specific knowledge represented in ontologies is used to improve the processing of user interventions in a multilingual dialogue system for multiple applications. The user interventions are processed by a left-corner parser performing syntactic and semantic analysis in parallel. The parser uses application-restricted grammars and lexicons obtained from ontologies representing the application specific knowledge. It also uses the knowledge of the dialogue context to select the grammar rules related to the dialogue focus.

1 Introduction

Many works have focused on the study of approaches that improve parsing in real-world applications. Several of these approaches propose new mechanisms to practical parsing speed-ups (Boullier, 2003), while others propose the use of semantic information to improve the parsing results (Mohanty and Balabantaray, 2003). This paper describes how the performance of a left-corner parser used in a practical dialogue system is improved by using knowledge from domain ontologies and context dialogue.

The Principle of Compositionality states that the meaning of a sentence can be composed of the meaning of its syntactic constituents. There are two different approaches following this principle: a pipeline architecture where the result of the parsing is passed as input to the semantic analyzer, and the integration of semantics directly into the parser. In this second approach, when performing syntactic and semantic analysis in parallel, the representation of the meaning for a constituent is created once all its constituent parts have been recognized. The main advantage of this approach is that semantic considerations can be used to reduce the number of possible syntactic structures to be considered.

However, the integration of semantic and syntactic analysis has also disadvantages. The primary of them being that considerable effort is spent on the semantic analysis of constituents that, in the end, do not contribute to a successful parse. Additionally, the traditional wide-coverage grammars are not particularly well-suited for compositional semantic analysis because they include many general syntactic constituents with no semantic role. For these reasons, many practical systems requiring semantic analysis for a particular domain use grammars adapted to the specific domain. As explained in (Jurafsky and Martin, 2000), these grammars simplify semantic processing in several ways:

- Their rules and constituents are designed to correspond directly to entities and relations from the domain.
- The key semantic components occur together within single rules while in traditional grammars the key semantic elements are often widely distributed across parse trees.
- Their nature enables a certain amount of prediction about upcoming input, thus helping with anaphor and ellipsis phenomena.

However, domain-restricted grammars and lexicon present several limitations. The possible sentences that can be analyzed correctly with domain-restricted resources are limited. Besides, the number of grammar rules needed for a particular domain can be high because syntactic generalizations are limited. Furthermore, application-restricted resources are expensive to develop and difficult to reuse.

This paper describes the approach followed when applying syntax-driven semantics to a practical dialogue system for multiple applications. This system supports speech and textual interaction in several languages (English, Spanish, Catalan and Italian). The voice components of the system are based on VoiceXML. The automatic speech recognition system uses grammars to recognize and process user interventions. These grammars incorporate semantic information (following the standard Speech Recognition Grammar Specification). The text input is processed by a chart-based parser, implemented in Prolog, with top-down filtering that performs the syntactic and semantic analyses in parallel. A more detailed description of it can be found in (Gatius, 2001).

In this dialogue system the application knowledge involved in the communication is represented in ontologies. These ontologies are used to generate the dialogues, the system messages and the linguistic structures necessary for processing user interventions. In this paper we focus on how the application specific knowledge represented in ontologies is used to improve the performance of the parser.

In the current implementation of the dialogue system the parser is only used to process text input. Basically, it is used to study how the voice module could be improved. For this reason, the grammars and lexicons used by the parser to process textual input are very similar to those used by the speech recognizer. For the next version of the system we are planning to integrate the parser with the voice module, using the last VoiceXML version.

As to the structure of this paper it is as follows: in the following section we describe the use of ontologies modelling the application tasks-specific knowledge for dialogue management. Section 3 describes how the application information represented in the ontologies is associated with the linguistic resources and how this information is used by the parser to interpret the user's interventions. Section 4 explains how the contextual information is used to improve the efficiency of the parser. Results of the parser performance are discussed in Section 5. And finally, the last section draws some conclusions.

2 Ontologies and Dialogue Management

Dialogue management techniques deal with the use of dialogue in furthering the user's objectives. Dialogue management is related to the type of interaction allowed, as well as the underlying task and domain.

This section describes briefly the different approaches to dialogue management according to how task models and dialogue models are used. Then it describes the approach followed by the dialogue system presented in the introduction, that is, the use of ontologies for modelling the application tasks. The following sections describe how these ontologies are used to improve the processing of user's interventions.

2.1 Dialogue Management Models

Almost all dialogue systems use a dialogue management model defining the dialogue control and guidance, although in many of them this model is not explicit. Dialogue management models have evolved from simple finite state automata, representing the questions asked by the system and all the actions to take depending on the user's response, to more complex models using dialogue and tasks models to provide generic behaviour.

The most simple dialogue management models are finite state models. They are still used in many spoken systems. In these models both dialogue model and task model are implicit. They are appropriate for simple and structured tasks but not for complex applications, when the number of possible interaction paths grows.

Many spoken question-answering systems use a more flexible dialogue management model, based on frames (or templates) representing the task model. These frames contain slots describing the various kinds of information the user would be asked to fill. The number of frames needed depends on the application tasks complexity. In most of those systems there is no explicit dialogue model. Frame-based system models are appropriate when the set of actions the system can do is reduced (being the number of frames limited), which is not the case in complex applications. The main problem in finite state and frame-based models is that they only support very limited user initiative.

In more complex systems a more flexible communication is provided by including explicit dialogue model as well as task model. Several dialogue systems supporting flexible communication in complex domain also include an explicit representation of the domain model. An example of a system using a dialogue model, a task model and a domain model is described in [9]. In this system, the intentional structure underlying the dialogue is derived from an ontology modelling the application tasks and the informational structure is obtained from the domain ontologies.

One of the advantages of using ontologies for representing the application tasks in comparison to other conceptual representations, such as frames, is that in ontologies relations and preconditions between different entities are defined. Therefore, ontologies allow more flexible dialogues. The use of ontologies has proved especially appropriate for dialogue systems supporting different languages and modes (Wahlster, 2003). In those systems the semantic interpretation of the user's intervention is represented in basis of the same ontology (independently of the mode and the language).

An additional benefit of using ontologies is that they facilitate the reuse of knowledge common to different applications, such as tasks obtaining personal data (address, telephone number, etc.).

2.2 Ontologies for Modelling the Application Task-specific Knowledge

The dialogue system we present uses ontologies representing the tasks models. This system (as most existing dialogue system) is driven by specific goals or tasks: finding a particular piece of information (informational dialogues) or executing a particular transaction (transactional dialogues). These tasks can be decomposed into hierarchically ordered subtasks. We proposed the representation of these tasks in ontologies improves the communication.

The dialogue system supports task-oriented dialogues. In these dialogues the application-dependent knowledge appearing in communication is related basically to the tasks the application can perform, that is, the information required to perform the task and the information resulting from it. Mainly, this information is related to the application parameters. This information can be represented by an ontology. In this ontology, all application tasks are represented by a set of concepts described by attributes. Basically, these attributes describe the input and output parameters. Preconditions governing in which context a particular attribute value must be asked to the user can also be included.

The dialogue manager uses this ontology to control both the interactions with the user and the access to the application back-end. The system asks the user to introduce the data required by the application at each state of the communication. Dialogue interactions consist mainly in asking and giving the values of the conceptual attributes describing the application tasks.

Using the ontologies describing the application-specific tasks the system supports different types of dialogues. It will drive the interaction asking inexperienced users all the information the application needs (represented as attributes describing the application tasks). Experience users can take the initiative and give specific information. Then, considering context dialogue and preconditions in the concepts descriptions, the dialogue manager will decide which specific data is needed from the user. If additional data is required, the system will ask for it. If a user's answer gives information not only about the attribute she is asked for but also about other attributes, this information will be kept and will not be asked in future interventions.

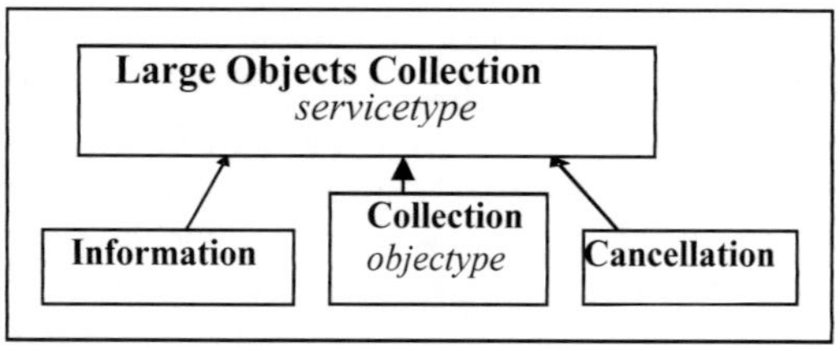

Figure 1. A fragment of the application Large Objects Collection

Figure 1 shows a fragment of the ontology representing the application to set a date to collect objects from homes. It is a transactional application performing three tasks: gives information, sets a date for collection and cancels collections previously arranged. Following the application description in Figure 1 the dialogue system will first ask the user the particular task she/he is interested in (i.e., *Say what you want, information, collection or cancellation*). If the user wants to set a data for collection, the dialogue system will then ask the type of object that has to be collected.

In complex and changing domains further improvements in communication can be achieved by using ontologies describing the domain-specific knowledge. Ontologies describing domain concepts and relations can be used for reasoning. Simple inferences, whether a class can be related to another by the *isa*-relation or other relations, such as part-whole, can help the system to detect differences in expectation in the user's interventions, such as under/over specification (corresponding to hyperonym or hypononym).
In current implementation domain, ontologies are only used to obtain all possible values of specific concept attributes, as explained in next section.

3 Using Ontologies for processing user's interventions

The advantages of using ontologies to relate the application specific knowledge to the linguistic resources needed in communication in multiple domain dialogue systems have been studied in several works (Dzikovska et al., 2003). This section describes the approach we follow to associate the information in the application-specific ontologies with the corresponding linguistic resources and how it is used by the parser to interpret the user's interventions.

3.1 The semantic analysis

The semantic analysis is based on *lambda calculus*. Semantic information is associated with each grammar rule to indicate the order of interpretation of its constituents. This information consists of a list of numbers representing the constituents. Figure 2 shows examples of application-restricted grammar rules together with their semantic interpretation. This semantic interpretation associated with each lexical entry consists of a lambda function or a lambda value. Figure 3 shows examples of lexical entries and their interpretation.

At run-time, once the parser has recognized all constituents of the rule, they are analyzed semantically. The semantic analysis consists in applying the semantic interpretation associated with the categories (the *lambda functions* over the *lambda values*) following the order indicated in the semantic list associated with the rule. The resulting semantic information is incorporated into the state stored in the chart. The semantic interpretation process returns a list of possible interpretations that will be passed to the dialogue component.

The semantic interpretation built by the parser will subsequently be passed to the dialogue manager. By using the application-restricted grammar and lexicon the parser obtains the semantic interpretations in the form needed by the dialogue manager. Each possible semantic interpretation is a list of words containing the identifiers of the ontology concepts, their attributes and values. Basically, this information represents the application operations, their parameters and values. Finally, the dialogue manager will complete the information in order to perform the corresponding actions (asking the user or accessing the application back-end).

3.2 The application-specific information associated with linguistic resources

The linguistic resources for each language consist of a general grammar and a general lexicon to process expressions common to all applications and application-specific grammars and lexicon. The application-restricted linguistic resources cover the expression of the entities in the ontologies representing the application tasks. The lexical entries expressing the concepts, attributes and their values are associated with their corresponding identifiers. In order to facilitate reusability, the linguistic resources expressing parameters appearing in more than one application (i.e., dates and addresses) are incorporated into the general grammar and general lexicon.

Examples of the linguistic resources obtained from the application description in Figure 1 are shown in Figure 2, Figure 3 and Figure 4. Figure 2 shows examples of the grammar rules used to process the user's answers when the dialogue system asks the two attributes (*servicetype* and *objectype*). The lexical entries appearing in those rules are shown in Figure 3 and Figure 4.

```
gramservicetype -> ncollection
gramobjectype -> nobjection
gramobjectype -> ncollection prepof ngobject (2(1 3))
ngobject -> number objectype (1 2)
ngobject -> objectype
```

Figure 2. Examples of grammar rules

Category	Interpretation	String
ncollection	(servicetype, collection)	collection
prepof	(((l,X),(l,Y)),(X,Y))	of

Figure 3. Examples of lexical entries

The linguistic resources built for the first prototype of the system are limited. We had decided to use grammars and lexicon that could automatically be represented in the voice grammars (following the standard Speech Recognition Grammar Specification). For this purpose, the information associated with the lexical entries is very simple.

We considered the key semantic information is that provided by the expression of the ontology concepts, their attributes and values. For this reason, the semantic representation associated with a lexical entry expressing these entities is a lambda value. In the case of concepts and attributes lambda values are represented by the identifiers of the corresponding concepts or attributes. The lambda value associated with the lexical entries expressing the value of conceptual attributes is represented by a list containing the attribute identifier and the value identifier. This information can be obtained automatically from the conceptual attributes in the ontology. The lexical entries not expressing relevant information for the application are associated with a lambda function over one or more lambda values.

Figure 3 shows two examples of lexical entries together with their semantic interpretation. The two lexical entries consist of three fields: category, semantic interpretation and string (or linguistic realization). The first lexical entry corresponds to the noun *collection*, expressing the service *collection*. The interpretation associated with this noun is a lambda value obtained from the ontology. This interpretation indicates that the noun *collection* expresses that the value of the attribute *servicetype* is the concept that has as identifier *collection*.

The second lexical entry in Figure 3 corresponds to the preposition *of*. This entry belongs to the general lexicon. The semantic interpretation associated with this preposition is a lambda function represented by the list *(((l,X),(l,Y)), (X,Y))*. The first sublist indicates that the function has two lambda arguments, represented by the variables *X* and *Y*. The second sublist establishes that the function returns a list containing the value of the two variables. This semantic interpretation indicates that the preposition *of* acts as a link between two semantic values.

The dynamic entries

Category	Dynamic function
number	integer
objectype	member(objectype)

Figure 4. Examples of dynamic entries

In order to improve the efficiency and friendliness of the communication we have incorporated dynamic categories. Their superficial representation, as well as the semantic interpretation associated with them, is set at run-time. The use of dynamic entries reduces the number of lexical entries to be considered and allows the user to introduce new values. Dynamic entries consist of two fields: the linguistic category and the dynamic function. At run-time the dynamic function processes the word(s) introduced by the user and returns the corresponding semantic information. There are two different types of dynamic entries: those representing open values (such as numbers, dates and telephone numbers) and those associated with a list of values (i.e., locations).

The first lexical entry in Figure 4 is an example of dynamic entry representing an open value. This lexical entry represents a number and is associated with the prolog predicate *integer*. The number expressed by the user would be associated with a lambda value represented by the word *number* and the numeric value. Entries representing open values can be associated with specific functions controlling the correctness of the values introduced by the user (i.e., dates, telephone numbers).

The second lexical entry in Figure 4 is an example of entry associated with a list of values. The main advantage of this way of representing the entries is that the list of values can easily be changed when there is a change in the application. It can be changed even at run-time. Another advantage of using entries associated with a list is that if the number of values is reduced those values can be presented as a menu at run-time. Then, the user has to choose only one or more values in the menu.

The dynamic entry *objectype* represents the object that has to be collected, that is, the possible values of the attribute *objectype* of the concept *Collection* in Figure 1. The function associated with the entry controls that the value introduced by the user corresponds to an element in the list *objectype*, containing the linguistic realization of the possible types of objects that could be collected.

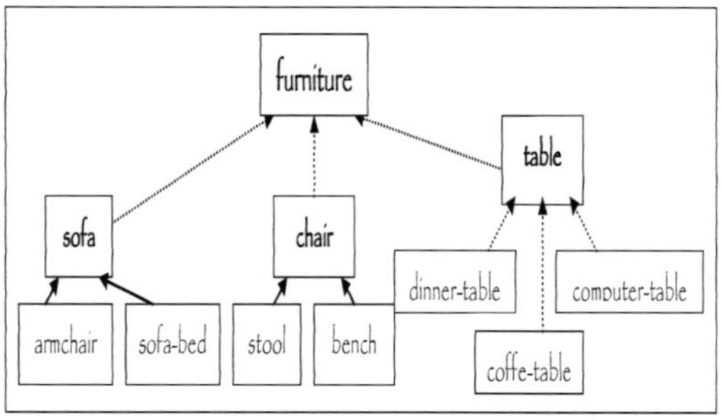

Figure 5. A fragment of the furniture taxonomy

To obtain the different types of objects we have used two existing taxonomies: one classifying different kinds of furniture, the other classifying different kinds of appliance. A fragment of the furniture taxonomy can be seen in Figure 5. For each language, the appropriate words and idioms expressing terms in those domain taxonomies have been incorporated into the list *objectype*. In the current implementation the list contains 321 entries for English, 277 for Spanish and 225 for Catalan.

4 Using context knowledge to improve efficiency

Linguistic resources adapted to the application have proved efficient when the sentences introduced by the user are limited to those supported by the grammar and lexicon. For this reason, they are specially appropriate for application-driven dialogues, where the system guides the user to introduce the data needed by the application. However, application-restricted resources can present limitations because they do not cover all possible sentences introduced by users, not even the most common mistakes.

To improve robustness the parser incorporates a garbage mechanism that eliminates all words in the user's interventions that are not covered by the linguistic resources. This garbage mechanism allows the parser to deal with spelling mistakes, ill-constructed sentences and correct sentences not covered by the domain-restricted grammars. However, it decreases the efficiency because it introduces ambiguity (different words in the user sentences can be considered "garbage") and some possibilities can lead to incorrect analyses (not corresponding to the meaning of the sentences stated by the user).

In order to limit the number of possible interpretations the parser takes advantage of the knowledge of the dialogue context. The parser obtains the text introduced by the user together with the dialogue focus. The dialogue focus consists of the attributes of the ontology concepts that have been previously asked to the user. As mentioned in Section 2, the dialogue manager uses the application specification represented in the ontology to ask the user the information needed by the application, that is, the value of the attributes describing the ontology concepts.

The approach we follow differs from that in other research dialogue systems supporting flexible communication. In dialogue systems such as (Traum et al., 1999; Meza-Ruiz and Lemon, 2005) different type of information related to the dialogue state is used to select the best hypothesis produced by the parser. This information could include current and past dialogue moves, questions under discussion, the tasks recently introduced in the dialogue, etc.

Our approach is related to that followed in many practical voice systems using VoiceXML. In the standard VoiceXML formalism the system prompt in an interaction is associated with the grammar(s) covering the next user's utterances expected. The grammar modelling the expected answer is then used by the voice engine to recognize the user's utterance. This approach has been applied successfully in practical voice systems because those systems support mainly system-driven dialogues.

In our approach the dialogue focus (the context of previous system messages) is used to give priority to the grammar rules representing the most probable user interventions in a particular state of the communication. The use of this information limits the number of rules that has to be considered at run-time and thus, it reduces ambiguity, it prevents the parser from performing semantic interpretations not useful. For this reason the run-time requirements decrease and the number of correct interpretations the parser passes to the dialogue manager (as the first correct interpretation in the list of possible interpretations) increases.

Only in the case that the user's sentence cannot successfully be analyzed using the set of rules selected, the parser would use the rest of the grammar to perform the analysis.

The selection of all grammar rules that can be involved in the expression of the information expected (the values of the attributes the system had asked the user) can be done easily because application-restricted grammars are used. In these grammars the left-hand part of the rules expressing the value of a specific attribute is represented by a category containing the prefix *gram* and the attribute identifier (i.e., in the examples shown in Figure 2 the category *gramservicetype* is the left-hand part of the grammar rule expressing the value of the attribute *servicetype* and *gramobjectype* is the left-hand part of the rules representing the *objectype* attribute).

Then, all rules that are reachable from those containing the attribute identifier in the left-hand are also selected. This process is done by applying the same top-down filtering used to select the appropriate grammar rules when processing text input. As mentioned before, the bottom-up parser uses a top-down filtering to improve efficiency. This filtering process is based on the data structure representing all reachable categories from the left-corner categories. This data structure is built previously to the analysis process.

For example, let's consider that the grammar consists of the rules in Figure 2. If the focus is *servicetype* only the first grammar rule would be selected. In the case the focus is *objectype* all rules except the first one would be selected.

5 Results and discussion

Tests have been done to compare results obtained by the parser when using the context dialogue to those obtained without this knowledge. We use the metrics precision and run-time requirements to evaluate the performance of the parser.

We have tested the parser using the grammars developed for two applications: The large Objects Collections and the Cultural Agenda, giving information about the cultural events. These grammars have been developed for three languages: English (164 rules, 437 lexical entries, 15 of them dynamic entries), Spanish (79 rules, 221 lexical entries, 15 of them dynamic) and Catalan (the translation of the rules and entries for Spanish).

In our experiments for each language we used 75 sentences introduced for a subject (native-speaker of Spanish and Catalan) not involved in the parser development. The subject answered the dialogue system prompts. The results obtained are shown in Table 1, Table 2 and Table 3. We calculated the precision of the parser results for each language. We considered the analysis of a sentence was correct when the first interpretation in the resulting list of possible interpretations was the correct one (the value of the attribute previously asked by the system). We also analyzed the decrease of the run-time requirements when using the dialogue context. We calculated the percentage of the sentences processed spending less run-time requirements (and analyzed correctly) when using context and the percentage when not using context.

	Using context	Not using context
Precision	94%	76%
Best run-time	60%	17,3%

Table 1: The parser evaluation for Spanish

	Using context	Not using context
Precision	84%	73,3%
Best run-time	45,3%	33,3%

Table 2: The parser evaluation for Catalan

	Using context	Not using context
Precision	77,3%	73,3%
Best run-time	48%	6,6%

Table 3: The parser evaluation for English

From these tables we can draw our first conclusion: using dialogue information improves precision and reduces the run-time requirements. The run-time for processing several sentences increases when context information is used. This is because selecting the grammars rules related to the dialogue focus implies some extra processing. Nevertheless, only if there is no possible ambiguity the processing without using dialogue context could be faster.

However, favouring those grammar rules expressing the answer expected by the system may limit the capabilities of the parser when processing unexpected statements. This is the case when the user's sentence gives information not only about the specific attribute the user is asked for but also about other relevant attributes. Let's consider, for example, the application for objects collection described in previous section. In order to obtain the value of the attribute *servicetype*, the system will ask "*Say what you want, information, collection or cancellation*". The user's answer could be *"Collection of two tables"*. Using context information, only the rules expressing the answer expected will be selected. In a reduced grammar those rules could only consider that the user can give information about the attribute *servicetype*. In that case, the parser would consider that the fragment *"of two tables"* is *garbage* and the resulting semantic interpretation would be *(servicetype collection)*. Then, the dialogue system would ask the user about the type of object to be collected (which could be boring for the user). In the case that all grammar rules would be considered (not only those expressing the answer expected) the whole user sentence could be correctly interpreted. For example, when using the third and fourth rules in Figure 2, the resulting semantic interpretation would be *((servicetype collection) (2, (objectype, table)))*.

In order to achieve efficient, robust and flexible communication context information must be used appropriately. Using context information to select a very limited set of rules for processing the answer expected could be useful when obtaining the value of relevant attributes (i.e., an account number) or in critical situations (when user's answers are not well understood). In other situations the context information would have to be used not only to favour the rules expressing the value of the attribute asked but also those expressing the value of other related attributes, such as those giving information about the same concept. In the example described above, both attributes *servicetype* and *objectype* give information about the concept *collection* and thus all the grammar rules related to its description would have to be selected (i.e. all the rules in

Figure 2 would be selected because all of them are related to the concept *collection*).

6 Conclusions and future work

In this paper we have described how the application specific knowledge represented in ontologies is used to improve the processing of user's interventions in a practical multilingual dialogue system for multiple applications. In this system the dialogues as well as the application-restricted resources are obtained from the ontologies representing the application specifications.

The use of ontologies has proved specially appropriate for dialogue systems in complex domains (complex concepts and relations) as well as for systems in multiple domains (information common to several applications can be easily reused) and in those systems supporting different modes of communication and languages (the semantic interpretation is represented in base to the same ontology).

We have described how a bottom-up parser uses the application specific knowledge associated with the lexical entries (obtained from the ontology representing the application) to process the user interventions. The resulting semantic interpretation is represented in base to the application specific ontology. In current implementation the semantics used to represent the application information associated with the lexical entries is very simple. For future prototypes we will study other forms of associating the application specific knowledge with the lexical entries.

In order to improve the performance the parser also uses the context dialogue. It uses information about previously asked questions (about the conceptual attribute values) to select the grammar rules related to the dialogue focus. The use of application specific and context knowledge improves both the run-time processing and the resulting semantic interpretation. However, in order to achieve a flexible communication context information must be used appropriately. Future improvements in the system will include considering different type of information related to the dialogue state.

We are planning to integrate the bottom-up parser with the voice module, using the last VoiceXML version. Future work will include comparing the results obtained when using the parser described to those obtained when using a statistical parser.

Although tests with real users have not been done yet, we expect the linguistic resources we have developed from applications specification would not cover the different ways users express themselves. For this reason, we are planning to test the current implementation of the system with different types of users and enriching the linguistic resources using the samples obtained. We are also planning to test the parser functionality in dialogues where users have more initiative.

Acknowledgements

This work has been partially supported by the EU IST FP6 project HOPS (IST-2002-507967).

We would like to thank Elisabet Comelles for her helpful comments.

References

Boullier, Pier. Guided Early Parsing. 8th International Workshop of Parsing Technologies, 2003.

Dzikovska, Myroslava. Allen, James F. and Swift, Mary. Finding the balance between generic and domain-specific knowledge: a parser customization strategy. 3rd Workshop on Knowledge and Reasoning in Practical Dialogue Systems, 2003.

Gatius, Marta. Using an ontology for guiding natural language interaction with knowledge based systems. Ph.D. thesis, Technical University of Catalonia. 2001. http://www.lsi.upc.es/~gatius/tesis.html.

Jurafsky, Daniel and Martin, James H. Speech and Language processing. Ed. Prentice-Hall, Inc. Pearson Higher Education, 2000.

Milward, David, Beveridge, M. Ontology-Based Dialogue Systems. In the Proceedings of the 3rd Workshop on Knowledge and Reasoning in Practical Dialogue Systems, 2003.

Meza-Ruiz, Ivan. and Lemon, Olivier. Using dialogue context to improve parsing performance in dialogue systems. International Workshop on Computational Semantics (IWCS), Tilburg, 2005.

Mohanty, Sanghamitra and Balabantaray, Rakesh Chandra. Intelligent parsing in Natural Language processing. 8th International Workshop of Parsing Technologies, 2003.

Traum, David, Bos, Johan, Cooper, Robin, Larson Staffan, Lewin, Ian, Mathesson, Colin, Poesio, Massimo. A model of Dialogue Moves and Information State Revision. Trindi Technical Report D2.1,1999.http://www.ling.gu.se/projekt/trindi//publications.html

Wahlster, Wolfgang . "SmartKom: Symmetric Multimodality in an Adaptive and Reusable Dialogue Shell". Proceedings of the Human Computer Interaction Status Conference, 2003.

Adjective based inference*

Marilisa Amoia
INRIA/Université de Nancy 1 &
University of the Saarland
Saarbrücken Germany
amoia@coli.uni-sb.de

Claire Gardent
CNRS/Loria
Campus Scientifique BP 239
54506 Vandoeuvre-les-Nancy, France
claire.gardent@loria.fr

Abstract

In this paper, we propose a fine grained classification of english adjectives geared at modeling the distinct inference patterns licensed by each adjective class. We show how it can be implemented in description logic and illustrate the predictions made by a series of examples. The proposal has been implemented using Description logic as a semantic representation language and the prediction verified using the DL theorem prover RACER.

Topics: Textual Entailment, Adjectival Semantics

1 Introduction

Understanding a text is one of the ultimate goals of computational linguistics. To achieve this goal, systems need to be developed which can construct a meaning representation for any given text and which furthermore, can reason about the meaning of a text. As is convincingly argued in (Ido Dagan and Magnini, 2005), one of the major inference task involved in that reasoning is the entailment recognition task:

Does text T_1 entail text T_2?

Indeed entailment recognition can be used to determine whether a text fragment answers a question (e.g., in question answering application), whether a query is entailed by a relevant document (in information retrieval), whether a text fragment entails a specific information nugget (in information extraction), etc.

Because the Pascal RTE challenge focuses on real text, the participating systems must be robust that is, they must be able to handle unconstrained input. Most systems therefore are based on statistical methods (e.g., stochastic parsing and lexical distance or word overlap for semantic similarity) and few provide for a principled integration of lexical and compositional semantics. On the other hand, one of the participant teams has shown that roughly 50% of the RTE cases could be handled correctly by a system that would adequately cover semantic entailments that are either syntax based (e.g., active/passive) or lexical semantics based (e.g., bicycle/bike). Given that the overall system accuracies hovered between 50 and 60 percent with a baseline of 50 %[1], this suggests that a better integration of syntax, compositional and lexical semantics might improve entailment recognition accuracy.

In this paper, we consider the case of adjectives and, building on approaches like those described in (Raskin and Nirenburg, 1995; Peters and Peters, 2000), we propose a classification of adjectives which can account for the entailment patterns that are supported by the interaction of their lexical and of their compositional semantics. We start by defining a classification schema for adjectives based on their syntactic and semantic properties. We then associate with each class a set of axioms schemas which translate the knowledge about lexical relations (i.e. antonymy) the adjectives of the class are involved in by extracting this information from WordNet (Miller, 1998) and a set of semantic construction rules and we show that these correctly predicts the observed entailment patterns. For instance, the approach will account for the following (non)-entailment cases:

(1) a. John frightened the child
$\models$ The child is afraid

*We thank la Région Lorraine, INRIA and the University of Sarrebruecken for partially funding the research presented in this paper.

[1] 50% of the cases were true entailment and 50% were false ones, hence tossing a coin would get half of the cases right.

b. Peter claims that John is a murderer
$\models$ John is an alledged murderer
$\not\models$ John is a murderer

c. This is a fake bicycle
$\models$ This is a false bike
$\models$ This is not a real bike
$\not\models$ This is a bike

d. John is not awake
$\models$ John sleeps
$\not\models$ John does not sleep

The approach is implemented using Description Logic as a semantic representation language and tested on a hand-built semantic test suite of approximately 1 000 items. In the latter part of the paper we discuss this testsuite and the philosophy behind it.

2 A fine grained classification for adjectives

As mentioned above, we propose a classification of adjectives based on their lexical, their model theoretic and their morpho-derivational properties. To facilitate the link with compositional semantics (the construction of a meaning representation for sentences containing adjectives), we also take into account syntactic properties such as the predicative/attributive or the static/dynamic distinction. We now detail each of these properties. The overall categorisation system is given in Figure 1.

2.1 Model theoretic properties

The main criteria for classification are given by (Kamp, 1975; Kamp and Partee, 1995) semantic classification of adjectives which is based on whether it is possible to infer from the Adj+N combination the Adj or the N denotation.
Intersective adjectives (e.g., *red*) licence the following inference inference patterns:

$$A + N \models A$$

$$A + N \models N$$

For instance, if *X is a red car* then *X is a car* and *X is red*
Subsective adjectives (e.g., *big*) licence the following inference pattern:

$$A + N \models N$$

For instance, if *X is a big mouse*, then *X is a mouse* but it is not necessarily true *X is big*
Privative adjectives licence the inference pattern:

$$A + N \models \neg N$$

For instance, if *X is a fake gun* then *X is not a gun*
Plain non-subsective adjectives (e.g., *alledged*) do not licence any inference
For instance, if *X is an alleged murderer* then it is unknown whether *X is a murderer or not*

2.2 Lexical semantics

From the lexical semantics literature, we take one additional classification criterion namely antonymy. As described in (Cruse, 1986), this term covers different kinds of opposite polarity relations between adjectives namly, binary opposition, contraries and multiple oppositions.
Binary oppositions covers pairs such as *wet/dry* which license the following inference pattern:

$$A1 \equiv \neg A2 \ \wedge \ \neg A1 \equiv A2$$

So that in particular:
$wet \equiv \neg dry \ \wedge \ \neg wet \equiv dry$
Contraries are pairs such as *long/short* where the implication is unidirectional:

$$A1 \models \neg A2 \ \wedge \ \neg A1 \not\models A2$$

$$A2 \models \neg A1 \ \wedge \ \neg A2 \not\models A1$$

and in particular:
$long \models \neg short \wedge \neg long \not\models short$
$short \models \neg long \wedge \neg short \not\models long$
Multiple oppositions involve a finite set of adjectives (e.g., *linguistic/economic/mathematical/...*) which are pairwise mutually exclusive. For a set of opposed adjectives $A_1 \ldots A_n$, the following axioms schemas will be licensed:

$$\forall i, j \ s.t. \ 1 \leq i, j \leq and \ i \neq j$$
$$A_i \models \neg A_j \quad and \quad \neg A_i \not\models A_j$$

2.2.1 Derivational morphology

We also take into account related forms that is, whether there exists a verb (V_a) or a noun that is semantically related to the adjectives being considered. Moreover, for nominalizations we distinguish whether the morphologically related noun is an event noun (N_e), a noun denoting a theta role of the related verb (N_θ) or a non-event noun (N_a).

As we shall see, this permits capturing entailment relations between sentences containing morphoderivational variants such as for instance :

(2) a. John is asleep (Adj $\rightarrow$ V_a)
$\models$ John sleeps

b. John is absent (Adj $\rightarrow$ N_θ)
$\models$ John is the absentee

c. John is deeply asleep (Adj $\rightarrow$ N_e)
$\models$ John's sleep is deep

2.2.2 Syntactic properties

To better support the syntax/semantic interface, we refine the adjectives classes distinguishable on the basis of the above criteria with the following syntactic ones taken from (Quirk et al., 1985).

Attributiveness/Predicativeness. English adjectives can be divided in adjectives which can be used only predicatively (such as *alone*), adjectives which can be used only attributively (such as *mechanical* in *mechanical enginner*) and adjectives which can be used in both constructions such as *red*.

Modifiability by *very*. We distinguish between adjectives such as *nice* which can be modified by *very* (i.e. *very nice*) and adjectives such as *alleged* which cannot (**very alleged*).

Gradability. We distinguish between adjectives such as *big* which express gradable properties and have comparative and superlative forms (*bigger, biggest*) and adjectives such as *rectangular* which don't (**more rectangular*).

Staticity/Dynamicity. Dynamic adjectives can be used in imperative constructions and in the progressive form (*Be reasonable, He is being reasonable*), static adjectives cannot (**Be short, He is being short*).

3 Semantic Classes and textual entailment recognition

In order to build our classification, we have analysed a set of about 300 english adjectives each of which was manually mapped to the WordNet synset correspondent to the more frequent meaning of the adjective. In some case, when an adjective presents polysemic forms which belong to different semantic classes more than one form has been considered. For example, for the adjective *civil* we consider two senses/forms $civil_1$ (synonym of *polite*, as in *civil man*) and $civil_2$ (as in *civil engineer*) which belong to different semantic classes, the first being intersective and the second subsective. As Figure 1 shows, the proposed classification includes 15 adjective classes, each with distinct syntactic and semantic properties.

To account for these differences, we define for each class a set of axiom schemas capturing the model theoretic, lexical semantics and morpho-derivational properties of that class. Lexical semantics and morpho-derivational information are derived from WordNet. For example, the axioms describing antonymy are obtained by extracting from WordNet the antonyms of a particular adjective and then by considering the direction of the entailment relevant for the class the adjective belongs to:

$$asleep \equiv wake \text{ vs. } polite \sqsubset rude$$

Morpho-derivational information are derived from WordNet by extracting the derivationally related forms for the given adjective and then iterating the extraction on nouns and verbs in order to obtain information about their antonyms and hyponyms. For scalar adjective like *tall*, WordNet contains also a relation `is_a_value_of` which offers a pointer to the noun concept the adjective is a value of. Moreover, WordNet links the noun concept to a list of attributes which describe the scalar property it represents. For example, the adjective *tall* is a value of $\{stature, height\}$ and `attributes of` $\{stature, height\}$ are *tall* and *short*.

Based on some basic syntactic patterns, we then show that these axioms predict the observed textual entailment patterns for that class.

Before we illustrate this approach by means of some example, we first show how we capture logical entailment between NL semantic representations in a description logic setting.

3.1 Using description logic to check entailment between NL sentences

As argued in (Gardent and Jacquey, 2003), description logic (DL) is an intuitive framework within which to perform lexical reasoning: it is efficient (basic versions of description logics are decidable), it is tailored to reason about complex taxonomies (taxonomies of descriptions) and it is equipped with powerful, freely available automated provers (such as RACER, (Volker Haarslev, 2001)). For these reasons, we are here exploring a DL encoding of the entailment recognition task for the set of examples we are considering.The particular language we assume has the following syntax.

$$C, D \rightarrow A|\top|\bot|\neg A \mid C \sqcap D \mid C \sqcup D \mid \forall R.C \mid \exists R.C$$

The semantics of this language is given below with Δ the domain of interpretation and I the interpretation function which assigns to every atomic con-

Adjective Class	Predicative/Attributive	Modifiable by *very*	Gradability	static/dynamic	Antonymy	Related forms	Semantic class
Class 1: *afloat*	predicative-only	-	-	static	multi-opposition	V_a, N_e, N_θ	intersective
Class 2: *asleep*	predicative-only	+	-	static	binary-opposition	V_a, N_e, N_θ	intersective
Class 3: *polite*	both	+	+	dynamic	contraries	N_a	intersective
Class 4: *dry*	both	+	+	static	binary-opposition	V_a, N_e, N_θ	intersective
Class 5: *open*	both	-	-	dynamic	binary-opposition	V_a, N_e, N_θ	intersective
Class 6: *male*	both	-	-	static	multi-opposition	$N_a, N_e,$	intersective
Class 7: *authentic*	both	+	-	static	binary-opposition	N_e	intersective
Class 8: *big*	both	+	+	static	contraries	N_e	subsective
Class 9: *good*	both	+	+	dynamic	contraries	N_e	subsective
Class 10: *cultural*	attributive-only	-	-	static	multi-opposition	N_a	subsective
Class 11: *recent*	attributive-only	+	-	static	multi-opposition	N_e	subsective
Class 12: *fake*	both	-	-	static	binary-opposition	V_a,N_e	privative
Class 13: *former*	attributive-only	-	-	static	multi-opposition	-	privative
Class 14: *questionable*	both	+	-	static	contraries	V_a, N_e	plain non-subsective
Class 15: *alleged*	attributive-only	-	-	static	contraries	V_a	plain non-subsective

Figure 1: Classes of Adjectives

cept A, a set $A^I \subseteq \Delta$ and to every atomic role R a binary relation $R^I \subseteq \Delta \times \Delta$.

$$\begin{array}{rcl} \top^I & = & \Delta \\ \bot^I & = & \emptyset \\ (\neg A)^I & = & \Delta \backslash A^I \\ (C \sqcap D)^I & = & C^I \cap D^I \\ (C \sqcup D)^I & = & C^I \cup D^I \\ (\forall R.C)^I & = & \{a \in \Delta \mid \forall b(a,b) \in R^I \rightarrow b \in C^I\} \\ (\exists R.C)^I & = & \{a \in \Delta \mid \exists b \in C^I \wedge (a,b) \in R^I n\} \end{array}$$

Now one basic problem with using DL to check entailment between NL expressions, is that DL formulae are "directional" in that they refer to a given set of individuals. For instance the sentence *The boat is floating* might be represented by either of the two formulae given in 3 but these two formulae do not stand in an entailment relation (since they refer to different kind of objects namely floating event of a boat in 3a and boats that float in 3b).

(3) a. float $\sqcap\exists$theme.boat

b. boat $\sqcap\exists$theme^{-1}.float

To remedy this shortcoming, we introduce the notion of a *rotation*. Given a DL formula which only contains conjunction (disjunction is translated in DL as different formulas)

$$\Phi = \sqcap_{i=1,n} \text{Event}_i \sqcap_{j=1,m} \exists \text{R}_j.\text{Type}_j$$

a rotation of this formula is defined as:

1. Φ
2. $\forall j \in \{1, ..., m\}$:
$Type_j \sqcap \exists \text{R}_j^{-1}.(\sqcap_{i=1,n}\text{Event}_i \sqcap_{1<k<j,j<k<m} \exists \text{R}_k.\text{Type}_k)$

so that the formula:

$$\text{Event}_1 \sqcap \text{Event}_2 \sqcap ... \sqcap \text{Event}_n \sqcap\exists\text{R}_1.\text{Type}_1 \sqcap\exists\text{R}_2.\text{Type}_2 ... \sqcap\exists\text{R}_n.\text{Type}_n$$

corresponds to the following n Rotations each of which describe the same situation from the point of view of a particular type

0. Event $\sqcap\exists\text{R}_1.\text{Type}_1 \sqcap\exists\text{R}_2.\text{Type}_2 ... \sqcap\exists\text{R}_n.\text{Type}_n$
$\subseteq$ Event
1. $\text{Type}_1 \sqcap\exists\text{R}_1^{-1}.(\text{Event} \sqcap\exists\text{R}_2.\text{Type}_2 ... \sqcap\exists\text{R}_n.\text{Type}_n)$
$\subseteq \text{Type}_1$
2. $\text{Type}_2 \sqcap\exists\text{R}_2^{-1}.(\text{Event} \sqcap\exists\text{R}_1.\text{Type}_1 ... \sqcap\exists\text{R}_n.\text{Type}_n)$
$\subseteq \text{Type}_2$

...

n. $\text{Type}_n \sqcap\exists\text{R}_n^{-1}.(\text{Event} \sqcap\exists\text{R}_1.\text{Type}_1 ... \sqcap\exists\text{R}_{n-1}.\text{Type}_{n-1})$
$\subseteq \text{Type}_n$

So for example, the sentence *Mary knows that John is the inventor of the radio* will be represented as a predicate logic formula
$\exists x_1 mary(x_1) \wedge \exists x_2 john(x_2) \wedge \exists x_3 radio(x_3) \wedge \exists e_1 know(e_1) \wedge \exists agent(e_1, x_1) \wedge \exists topic(e_1, e_2) \wedge \exists e_2 invent(e_2) \wedge agent(e_2, x_2) \wedge patient(e_2, x_3)$
the denotation of this PL formula corresponds to the set of individuals $\{x_1, x_2, x_3\} \cup \{e_1, e_2\}$. The corresponding DL representation will be the underspecified representation
know $\sqcap\exists$ agent.mary $\sqcap\exists$ topic.(invent $\sqcap\exists$agent.john $\sqcap\exists$ patient.radio)
the denotation of which corresponds to the set $\{e_1\}$ and all its rotations which permit to access the other sets of individuals asserted in the sentence. Thus for example, the set $\{x_1\}$ which describes the individual *Mary* can be accessed through the following rotation:

$$\text{Rotation}_1\text{: mary} \sqcap\exists \text{ agent}^{-1}.(\text{know} \sqcap\exists \text{ topic.(invent} \sqcap\exists\text{agent.john} \sqcap\exists \text{ patient.radio))}$$

Finally, we say that an arbitrary formula/representation Φ_1 implies the formula Φ_2 iff it is possible to find a rotation $Rotation_i$ of Φ_1 the denotation of which describes a subset of the denotation of Φ_2:

Definition

$$\Phi_1 \models \Phi_2 \; iff \; \exists i.Rotation_i(\Phi_1) \sqsubseteq \Phi_2 \quad (1)$$

3.2 Example class axioms and derivations

We now illustrate our approach by looking at two classes in more detail namely, class 1 and class 8.

3.2.1 Class 1

Syntactically, Class 1 contains adjectives like *adrift,afloat,aground* which can only be used predicatively, are non gradable and cannot be modified by *very*. Semantically, they behave like intersective adjectives which enter in multiple opposition relations with other adjectives. They are furthermore morphologically derived from verbs and can be nominalized. To reflect these semantic properties we use the following axioms.

Model theoretic semantics. Adjectives of class 1 are intersective adjective. They will thus licence the correponding inference patterns namely:

$$A + N \models A \quad (2)$$

$$A + N \models N \quad (3)$$

Lexical semantics. Adjectives of class 1 enter in multiple opposition relations. Hence For instance:

afloat $\models \neg$ aground $\wedge \neg$ afloat $\not\models$ aground
aground $\models \neg$ afloat $\wedge \neg$ aground $\not\models$ afloat
sunken $\models \neg$ afloat $\wedge \neg$ afloat $\not\models$ sunken
afloat $\models \neg$ sunken $\wedge \neg$ sunken $\not\models$ afloat

Morpho-derivational semantics. Adjectives in Class 1 can be related to both nouns and verbs. Thus, for example the adjective *afloat* in WordNet is related to the noun *floating* which is related to the verb *float*, by assuming that the semantics assigned to the verb *float* is `float`(e), theme(e,a), the adjective *afloat* is assigned the following semantics:

afloat $\equiv \exists$ Theme^{-1}.float

This is encoded in the following axiom schemas:

MDR 1. Adj1 $\sqsubset \neg$ Adj2 If Adj1 = Anto(Adj2)
e.g., afloat $\sqsubset \neg$ sunken

MDR 2. Adj1 $\equiv \exists$ Theme^{-1}.V1 If Adj1 is related to V1
e.g.,afloat $\equiv \exists$ Theme^{-1}.float

MDR 3. V1 $\sqsubset \neg$ V2 If V1 = Anto(V2)
e.g., float $\sqsubset \neg$ sink

MDR 4. N1 $\equiv$ V1 If Adj1 is related to an evt denoting N1
e.g., floating $\equiv$ float

MDR 5. N1 $\sqsubset \neg$ N2 If N1 is an antonym of N2
e.g., floating $\sqsubset \neg$ sinking

MDR 6. N11 $\equiv \exists$ Theme^{-1}.V1 If Adj1 is related to a noun N11 denoting the theme role of the verb V1
e.g., floater $\equiv \exists$ Theme^{-1}.float

We make the following assumptions about the syntax/semantic interface that is, about the semantic representations associated with given sentence patterns.

SCR 1. NP toBe Adj
$ADJ \sqcap NP$

SCR 2. NP toBe clearly Adj
$ADJ \sqcap NP$

SCR 3. N_i[+event] of NP is clear
$V_i \sqcap \exists theme.NP$

SCR 4. N_{ii}[-event] is clear
$\exists theme^{-1}.V_i$

SCR 5. NP toBe V[+ing].
$V \sqcap \exists Theme.NP$

Given the above axiom schemas and semantic constructions rules, the following inference patterns can be handled:

1. ADJ1 + N $\models$ N
Ex. This boat is afloat. $\models$ This is a boat.
2. ADJ1 + N $\models$ ADJ1
Ex. This boat is afloat. $\models$ This is afloat.
3. ADJ1 + N $\not\models \neg$ N
Ex. The boat is afloat. $\not\models$ This not a boat.
4. ADJ1 + N $\models \neg$ ADJ2 $\sqcap$ N
Ex. The boat is afloat. $\models$ The boat is not sunken.
5. $\neg$ ADJ1 + N $\not\models$ ADJ2 $\sqcap$ N
Ex. The boat is not afloat. $\not\models$ The boat is sunken.
6. ADJ1 + N $\models$ N $\sqcap\exists$theme^{-1}.$V1$
Ex. The boat is afloat. $\models$ The boat is the floater.
7. ADJ1 + N $\models$ V1 $\sqcap\exists$theme.N
Ex. The boat is afloat. $\models$ The boat is floating.
8. ADJ1 + N $\models$ N1 $\sqcap\exists$theme.N
Ex. This boat is clearly afloat. $\models$ The floating of the boat is clear.
9. ADJ1 + N $\models$ N $\sqcap\exists$theme^{-1}.N1
Ex. This boat is clearly afloat. $\models$ The floating of the boat is clear (or the boat is the floating object).
10. $\neg$ (ADJ1 + N) $\models \neg$ (V1 $\sqcap\exists$theme.N) $\not\models \neg$ N
Ex. This is not a floating boat. $\not\models$ This is not a boat.
11. $\neg$ (ADJ1 + N) $\not\models \neg$ Adj1
Ex. This is not a floating boat. $\not\models$ This is not afloat.
12. $\neg$ (ADJ1 + N) $\not\models \neg$ V1
Ex. This is not a floating boat. $\not\models$ This is not floating.
13. $\neg$ (ADJ1 + N) $\not\models \neg$ N1
Ex. This is not a floating boat. $\not\models$ This is not a floating.
14. $\neg$ (ADJ1 + N) $\not\models \neg \exists$ theme^{-1}.V1
Ex. This is not a floating boat. $\not\models$ This is not the floater.
15. $\neg$ (ADJ1 + N) $\not\models \neg \exists$ theme.N
Ex. This is not a floating boat. $\not\models$ This is not a floating.

In the inference patterns 10 to 15, the negation of the adjective-noun compound $\neg$ (ADJ1 + N) is syntactically blocked, as the adjectives in this class are used predicative only, however the equivalent representation V1 $\sqcap\exists$theme.N can be used to motivate the inferences.

The following show in more detail how the first three of the above (non) entailments are recognised.

(4) a. The boat is afloat.

b. $\models$ The boat is floating.

4a	$\equiv$ Boat $\sqcap$ Afloat	(by SCR 1)	A
4b	$\equiv$ Float $\sqcap\exists Theme$.Boat	(by SCR 5)	B
Afloat	$\equiv \exists Theme^{-1}.Float$	(by MDR 2)	C
1	$\equiv$ Boat $\sqcap\exists Theme^{-1}.Float$	(from A and C)	D
	D $\models$ B	(By Defn 1)	E

(5) a. The boat is afloat.

b. $\models$ The boat is the floater.

5a	$\equiv$ Boat $\sqcap$ Afloat	(by SCR 1)	A
5b	$\equiv$ Boat $\sqcap\exists Theme^{-1}.float$	(by SCR 4)	B
Afloat	$\equiv \exists Theme^{-1}.Float$	(by MDR 2)	C
	A $\models$ B	(from B und C)	D

(6) a. The boat is afloat.

b. $\models$ The boat is not sinking.

6a	$\equiv$ Boat $\sqcap$ Afloat	(by SCR 1)	A
6b	$\equiv\neg$ sink $\sqcap\exists Theme.boat$	(by SCR 5)	B
Afloat	$\equiv \exists Theme^{-1}.Float$	(by MDR 2)	C
	Boat $\sqcap\exists Theme^{-1}.Float$	(from A and C)	D
	float $\sqcap\exists Theme.boat$	(By Defn 1)	E
	E $\models$ B	(by MDR 1)	F

3.2.2 Class 8.

Class 8 contains adjectives like *big,fast,tall,deep* which can be used attributively and predicatively, are gradable, can be modified by *very*. Semantically, they are classified as subsective adjectives and their antonyms are contraries. They are morphologically related to nouns which describe the particular property denoted by the adjectives and to nouns of which they are attributes.

Model theoretic semantics. Adjectives of class 8 are subsective adjective. They will thus licence the correponding inference patterns namely:

$$A + N \not\models A \quad (4)$$

$$A + N \models N \quad (5)$$

Lexical semantics. The Adjectives of class 8 enter in contrary opposition relations. Hence, the following axioms schemas will be licensed:

$$A_i \models \neg Anto(A_i) \quad and \quad \neg A_i \not\models Anto(A_i) \quad (6)$$

For instance:

long $\models\neg$ small $\wedge\neg$ long $\not\models$ small
deep $\models\neg$ shallow $\wedge\neg$ deep $\not\models$ shallow

Morpho-derivational semantics. Adjectives in Class 8 can be related to nouns but not to verbs. Moreover, such adjectives are mapped in WordNet to noun concepts through two different links: `derivationally_related_to` and `is_a_value_of`. For example, the adjective *tall* in WordNet is derivationally related to the noun *tallness* and is a value of the concept noun *height*. The adjectives in this class describe gradable properties so that their semantics corresponds to:

has-property(Related_Noun $\sqcap\exists$has-measure.Top)

in which the role `has-measure` account for the value of the scalar property described by the adjective, which remain underspecified (Top) if the adjective is used without a reference to the value of measure. When the value of the measure is specified, for example by combining the adjective with a noun, as for example in *This is a tall man*, then the noun is assigned as a value of the measure role:

man $\sqcap\exists$has-property.(tallness
$\sqcap\exists$has-measure.man)

which translate *This is tall as a man*.

This is encoded in the following axiom schemas:

MDR 1. Adj1 $\sqsubset\neg$ Adj2 If Adj1 = Anto(Adj2)
Ex. tall $\sqsubset\neg$ short

MDR 2. Adj1 $\sqsubset\exists$ has_property.(N1 $\sqcap\exists$has_measure.Top)
If Adj1 is related to a noun N1 denoting the property described by Adj1
Ex. tall $\sqsubset\exists$ has_property.(tallness $\sqcap\exists$has_measure.Top)

MDR 3. N1 $\sqsubset\neg$ N2 If N1=Anto(N2)
Ex. tallness $\sqsubset\neg$ shortness

MDR 4. N1 $\equiv$ N' $\sqcap\exists$has_value.Adj1
If Adj1 is an attribute of the noun N'
Ex. tallness $\equiv$ height $\sqcap\exists$has_value.tall

MDR 5. N2 $\equiv$ N' $\sqcap\exists$has_value.Adj2
If Adj2 is an attribute of the noun N'
Ex. shortness $\equiv$ height $\sqcap\exists$has_value.short

MDR 6. N1 $\sqsubset$ N' If N1 is an hyponym of N'
Ex. tallness $\sqsubset$ height

MDR 7. N2 ⊏ N' If N2 is an hyponym of N'
Ex. shortness ⊏ height

MDR 8. Adj11 ⊏ Adj1 If Adj1 is a scalar attribute with value less then Adj11 (hyponymy is not defined for adjectives)
Ex. giant ⊏ tall

For the moment, we don't account for the semantics of comparatives forms of adjectives but we will do that in the feature, by also introducing a representation for scales as described in (Kennedy, 2005).

We make the following assumptions about the semantic representations associated with basic sentence patterns.

SCR 1. NP toBe Adj
NP ⊓∃ has_property.(N1 ⊓∃has_measure.NP)

SCR 2. That toBe Det Adj NP
NP ⊓∃ has_property.(N1 ⊓∃has_measure.NP)

SCR 3. NP toBe clearly Adj
NP ⊓∃ has_property.(N1 ⊓∃has_measure.NP)

SCR 4. N1 of NP is clear
NP ⊓∃ has_property.(N1 ⊓∃has_measure.NP)

SCR 5. The Adj N' of NP
NP ⊓∃ has_property.(N' ⊓∃ has_value.Adj ⊓∃has_measure.NP)

SCR 6. NP1 toBe Adj as a N
NP1 ⊓ N ⊓∃has_property.(N' ⊓∃ value.Adj ⊓∃ has_measure.N)

SCR 7. NP1 toBe NP2[+measure] Adj
NP1 ⊓∃has_property.(N' ⊓∃ value.Adj ⊓∃ has_measure.NP2)

SCR 8. NP1 toBe NP2[+measure] Adj N
NP1 ⊓ N ⊓∃has_property.(N' ⊓∃has_value.Adj ⊓∃ has_measure.NP2)

Given the above axioms, the following examples can be handled:

(7) (a) John is a 1.50 meter tall man.
⊨ (b) John is 1.50 meter tall.

7a	≡ John ⊓ Man ⊓∃has_property.(height ⊓has_value.tall ⊓has_measure(1.50 meter)) (by SCR 8)	A
7b	⊨ John ⊓∃has_property.(height ⊓has_value.tall ⊓has_measure(1.50 meter)) (by SCR 7 and from A)	B
	A ⊨ B	C

(8) (a) John is a 1.50 meter tall man. ⊭ (b) John is a tall man.

8a	≡ John ⊓ Man ⊓∃has_property.(height ⊓has_value.tall ⊓has_measure(1.50 meter)) (by SCR 8)	A
8b	⊨ John ⊓ Man ⊓∃has_property.(height ⊓ has_value.tall ⊓has_measure(man)) (by SCR1 and from A)	B
	A ⊭ B	C

4 Implementation

For each of the 15 classes, we have specified a set of axioms schemas, some basic semantic construction rules and a set of inference patterns which could be deduced to follow from both of these. The axioms schemas were implemented in Description Logic using RACER and for each inference pattern identified, the corresponding Description Logic query was checked to verify that the proposed axioms and semantic construction rules did indeed correctly predict the deduced inference patterns.

5 Further work and evaluation

The main contribution of this work is a detailed analysis of the interactions between derivational morphology, lexical and compositional semantics and of their impact on the entailment patterns licensed by sentences containing adjective or their related nouns/verbs.

To turn this analysis into a computational system, its components need to be integrated into a semantic analyser and the behaviour of that analyser tested against a collection of data. We are currently working on developing such an analyser within a symbolic grammar framework. We have also started to develop an evaluation test suite geared towards entailment recognition between sentence pairs containing adjectives. At the moment, the test suite contains about 1 000 inference pairs. Each item in the TestSuite (see fig. 2) is annotated with a judgement about the truth of the entailment between the pair of sentences, with the type of inference involved and with the specification of adjective involved. Moreover, each adjective is annotated with the WordNet sense corresponding to the given class.

The idea behind this test suite is similar to that underlying the creation of the TSNLP (Test suite for natural language processing) (see (Oepen and Netter, 1995)) or the Eurotra testsuites (see (Arnold and des Tombe, 1987)) namely, to provide a benchmark against which to evaluate and compare existing semantic analyzers. Thus this

```
<pair id="1" value="TRUE" class="[CLASS1]" inference="Adj/Verb">
     <t>The boat is <sn n="1"> afloat </sn>.</t>
     <h>The boat is floating.</h>
</pair>
<pair id="2" value="FALSE" class="[CLASS6]" inference="Antonymy">
     <t>This is not a  <sn n="1"> rectangular </sn> table.</t>
     <h>This is a  <sn n="1"> round </sn> table </h>
</pair>
<pair id="3" value="TRUE" class="[CLASS8]" inference="Adj/Noun">
     <t>The line is 2 meter  <sn n="1"> long </sn>.</t>
     <h>The length of the line is 2 meter.</h>
</pair>
<pair id="4" value="FALSE" class "[subs/intersective]" inference="Attr/Pred">
     <t>The treasurer is  <sn n="2"> present </sn>.</t>
     <h>This is the  <sn n="1"> present </sn> treasurer.</h>
</pair>
```

Figure 2: TestSuite

test suite illustrates the semantic and syntactic behaviour of adjectives and their related verbs/nouns with respect to textual entailment. One could imagine other test suites illustrating the semantic behaviour of verbs, of quantifiers, of discourse connectives, etc. Just as the TSNLP still proves useful in supporting the development of new symbolic parsers/grammars, hand built test suites of artificial examples might prove useful in improving the accuracy of semantic analyser wrt textual entailment. Indeed the Pascal RTE challenge has shown that existing systems fares rather poortly at the textual entailment task. Providing a set of hand crafted semantic test suites might help in remedying this shortcoming.

Beside implementing and evaluating the analysis of adjectives presented in this paper, we are also working on refining this analysis by combining it with a detailed analysis of noun semantics so as to handle (non) entailments such as:

(9)

Lyon is the gastronomical capital of France
$\not\models$ Lyon is the capital of France

References

D.J. Arnold and Luis des Tombe. 1987. *Basic Theory and methodology in Eurotra*. Cambridge University Press.

DA. Cruse. 1986. *Lexical Semantics*. Cambridge University Press.

Claire Gardent and Evelyne Jacquey. 2003. Lexical reasoning. In *Proceedings of the ICON'03 (International Conference on Natural Language Processing)*, Mysore, India.

Oren Glickman Ido Dagan and Bernardo Magnini. 2005. *The PASCAL Recognising Textual Entailment Challenge*.

Hans Kamp and Barbara Partee. 1995. Prototype theory and compositionality. *Cognition*, (57):129–191.

Hans Kamp. 1975. Two theories about adjectives. In Edward L. Keenan (ed.), *Formal Semantics of Natural Language*, pages 123–155. Cambridge University Press.

Christofer Kennedy. 2005. Vagueness and grammar: The semantics of relative and absolute gradable adjectives. *Ms.*, pages 129–191, June.

K. J. Miller. 1998. Modifiers in wordnet. In C. Fellbaum (ed.), *WordNet An Electronic Lexical Database*. Cambridge, MA, The MIT Press.

Stephan Oepen and Klaus Netter. 1995. TSNLP - test suites for natural language processing. Groningen, The Netherlands. Conference on Linguistic Databases.

I. Peters and W. Peters. 2000. *The Treatment of Adjectives in SIMPLE: Theoretical Observations*. Athens.

R. Quirk, S. Greenbaum, G. Leech, and J. Svartvik. 1985. *A Comprehensive Grammar of the English Language*. Longman.

V. Raskin and S. Nirenburg. 1995. *Lexical Semantics of Adjectives, a micro-theory of adjectival meaning*. MCCS Report.

Ralf Möller Volker Haarslev. 2001. Description of the racer system and its applications. In *Proceedings International Workshop on Description Logics (DL-2001*, Stanford, USA.

Natural Language Understanding using Temporal Action Logic

Martin Magnusson
Department of Computer and Information Science
Linköping University, SE-581 83 Linköping, Sweden
email: marma@ida.liu.se
www.phlai.com/nl1

Abstract

We consider a logicist approach to natural language understanding based on the translation of a quasi-logical form into a temporal logic, explicitly constructed for the representation of action and change, and the subsequent reasoning about this semantic structure in the context of a background knowledge theory using automated theorem proving techniques. The approach is substantiated through a proof-of-concept question answering system implementation that uses a head-driven phrase structure grammar developed in the Linguistic Knowledge Builder to construct minimal recursion semantics structures which are translated into a Temporal Action Logic where both the SNARK automated theorem prover and the Allegro Prolog logic programming environment can be used for reasoning through an interchangeable compilation into first-order logic or logic programs respectively.

1 Introduction

A complex and poorly understood area in computational linguistics is the integration and use of background knowledge to aid parsing, interpretation and understanding of natural language. There is general agreement that background knowledge is needed, e.g. to select between ambiguous interpretations or to provide answers to questions, and that without at least a partial understanding of the world a system can never hope to approach full natural language understanding. As artificial intelligence research moves closer to applications there is an increasing risk that too many natural language projects concentrate on the robust performance that is required in real-world applications and that they, while realizing that background knowledge is important, tend to make its role peripheral instead of a solid base on which to build upon.

We describe a natural language understanding system based on a logicist knowledge representation foundation that serves as a research platform for experimentation with the interchange between computational linguistics and knowledge representation and reasoning. The focus is the representational and inferential adequacy of the underlying techniques, which have been selected for generality and extensibility, rather than on immediate applicability or the similarity with human dialogue characteristics. The techniques are brought together in a simple and clear architecture that holds great potential for development and experimentation. A novel integration of natural language technology, knowledge representation technology, and automated reasoning technology in a proof-of-concept question answering system, with the working title NL1, has been implemented and is available as open source[1].

2 Temporal Action Logic

The Temporal Action Logic (TAL) is a non-monotonic temporal logic developed specifically for reasoning about actions and dynamical domains. The logic has its origin in the Features and Fluents framework developed by Sandewall (1994) but was given a new characterization in terms of circumscription by Doherty (1994). Many extensions since have turned TAL into a very expressive language capable of representing, among other things, actions with durations,

[1] `http://www.phlai.com/nl1`

`per1`	$\forall t\,[Per(t, alive) \wedge Per(t, loaded)]$
`acs1`	$[t_1, t_2]\ Load \rightsquigarrow R((t_1, t_2]\ loaded)$
`acs2`	$[t_1, t_2]\ Fire \rightsquigarrow ([t_1]\ loaded \rightarrow R((t_1, t_2]\ \neg alive \wedge \neg loaded))$
`obs1`	$[0]\ \neg loaded \wedge alive$
`occ1`	$[1, 2]\ Load$
`occ2`	$[3, 4]\ Fire$

Figure 1: The Yale shooting scenario in TAL.

context-dependent and non-deterministic actions, concurrency, and action side-effects. It also provides solutions to the frame, ramification and qualification problems. For a more detailed introduction to TAL the reader is referred to (Doherty et al., 1998).

2.1 TAL Narratives

Domains are described in TAL using *fluents* that represent properties of the world that change over time. World laws governing the evolution of fluents are expressed in *narratives*, which are high-level descriptions of observations, action schemas, and action occurrences. Narratives receive a semantics through a translation to the base language, which is an order-sorted classical first-order logic together with a circumscription policy described below. Figure 1 shows the well-known Yale shooting scenario expressed as a TAL narrative. A persistence statement (labelled `per1`) constrains the fluents $alive$ and $loaded$'s values to persist unless they are affected by some action. Action schemas (`acs1` and `acs2`) use the reassignment operator R to make $loaded$ true after performing the $Load$ action and to make both $loaded$ and $alive$ false after performing the $Fire$ action, but only if $loaded$ was true when the action was initiated. An observation statement (`obs1`) initializes $loaded$ and $alive$ to false and true respectively. Finally, the two occurrence statements (`occ1` and `occ2`) describe a world history in which the $Load$ action is performed between time points 1 and 2, and the $Fire$ action is performed between 3 and 4.

2.2 Occlusion

The key to the solution of the frame problem in TAL lies in the use of *occlusion*. When narratives are translated into classical logic an $Occlude$ predicate is introduced and constrained to be true at those time points where fluents are forced to change their values due to reassignments. An additional *no-change* axiom is added that rules out any fluent changes at any time points when the fluent was not occluded. The final step is the minimization of the $Occlude$ predicate and the action occurrences, expressing the default assumption that no unexpected fluent changes or spurious actions occur unless explicitly specified. The minimization is accomplished through the circumscription of those parts of the translated theory that contain action schemas and action occurrences respectively.

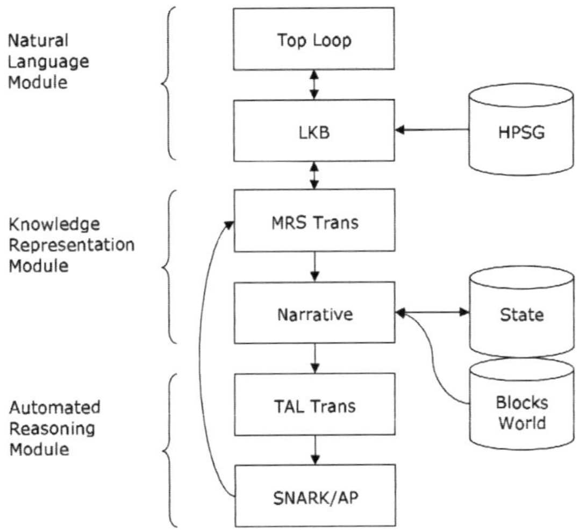

Figure 2: An overview of the NL1 architecture.

3 System Architecture

NL1 carries on an interactive natural language text dialogue with the user, executing commands and answering queries about a simulated blocksworld. An important emphasis of the system architecture, depicted in Figure 2, is the use of declarative knowledge structures in the hope of building a system that is both convenient to adapt to new usage scenarios and that has a great ultimate potential for extension while at the same time retaining the basic implementation components.

3.1 Natural Language Module

The natural language module is responsible for the parsing of input sentences and the construction of a quasi-logical form. User interaction consists of natural language input and output through a minimal user interface in the form of a text top-loop. Sentence are read from a prompt and passed as text strings to the Linguistic Knowledge Builder (LKB) component. The LKB chart parser uses a Head-driven Phrase Structure Grammar (HPSG), based on the grammar in (Sag et al., 2003), to parse the input text string and build a feature structure representation. The grammar includes semantical relations, and the semantical part of the feature structure representation constitutes a Minimal Recursion Semantics (MRS) structure.

One of the benefits of this set-up is that natural language generation can be achieved by running the chart parser "in reverse" using the same grammar that was used when parsing. The task of generating a response is then reduced to the task of constructing a suitable MRS structure representing an answer to the user's request.

The HPSG grammar forms a declarative knowledge source that is easily adapted to new vocabularies, by changing the lexicon of words and semantical relations, and that has a great potential for extension, e.g., moving towards broad coverage as in the English Resource Grammar project (Copestake and Flickinger, 2000).

3.2 Knowledge Representation Module

The knowledge representation module holds a representation of both the basic world laws and the particulars of the current scenario, but also a history of the developments of the world during the ongoing dialogue.

The world model, together with action specifications and an initial state is encoded as TAL formulas and stored in the blocksworld knowledge base. A continually evolving TAL narrative of action occurrences represents the world history and is stored in the state knowledge base. Any sentence that enters the system reaches the knowledge representation module in the form of an MRS structure that needs to be transformed into a full logical form before it is used in reasoning. The MRS structure is passed to the translation component that implements a partial translation by performing a number of transformations, as described in Section 4, that result in a TAL formula. If the natural language module identified the sentence as an imperative command, the TAL formula is appended to the narrative, but if the sentence was identified as a proposition or a question, a reasoning problem is formed by combining the corresponding TAL formula with the background blocksworld theory.

By using TAL as our knowledge representation language we are able to express a wide range of common-sense reasoning scenarios and ensure that the system is not limited to the relatively simple blocksworld, even though it is used as an illustrative example.

3.3 Automated Reasoning Module

Performing automated reasoning in the Temporal Action Logic is not trivial since it is a non-monotonic logic with a semantics based on circumscription. When Sandewall developed the basis of the formalism he was concerned more with assessing its correctness rather than performing automated reasoning. Later Doherty and Łukaszewicz (1994) showed how the semantics could be expressed using circumscription and, in (Doherty, 1994), that under certain restrictions the circumscription policy could be reduced to predicate completion (defined by Lifschitz (1994)) which is computable and results in an equivalent first-order characterization.

These methods open up the possibility of reasoning in TAL using a very flexible compilation approach that fits in nicely with the TAL high-level narrative description to base language translation. The idea is to choose an existing domain-independent automated reasoning paradigm and develop a compilation step from the TAL base language into a language compatible with that paradigm. The most obvious example would be a compilation into regular first-order logic and the application of resolution theorem provers, but other options are certainly possible as will be described below. The flexibility lies in the postponing of the expressibility vs. tractability tradeoff decision to the time at which some specific application domain is fixed, or even later, to the time at which a specific reasoning problem needs to be addressed. For example, one would like to detect if the theory is Horn and then use a logic program compilation while still retaining the possibility to automatically fall back to first-order or even higher-order logic if necessary. Such a classification of the complexity of the reasoning problem is not possible in general, but even an incomplete version might be tremendously useful in certain domains.

Our implementation includes two different compilation mechanisms. One results in a first-order theory that is further encapsulated (adding explicit theorem proving strategies and other configurations) to form an input problem to SNARK (Stickel, 2005), a resolution theorem prover with support for, among other things, sorts and answer

(1) B1 is on the table.
Ok.
(2) The table supports B1.
Yes.
(3) Does the table support B2?
I don't know.
(4) B2 is on the table and B3 is on B1.
Ok.
(5) Does the table support B3?
No.
(6) What blocks are clear?
B3 is clear and B2 is clear.
(7) Pick up B3.
Ok.
(8) Put B3 on the table.
Ok.
(9) What blocks are on the table?
B2 is on the table and B1 is on the table and B3 is on the table.

Figure 3: An example dialogue from NL1.

extraction. The other compilation results in a logic program that is further specialized into a program for Allegro Prolog[2], a Prolog environment that is fully integrated in the Allegro Common-Lisp development environment. In both cases, depending on the question type, the result is the deduction of true or false, or the extraction of answer terms from a proof of the query formula. These answer formulas are passed back to the natural language module where they are used in the construction of an answer MRS that generates a natural language response, closing the loop.

3.4 Example Dialogue

The example dialogue in Figure 3 illustrates the working system and consists of numbered interactions between an operator and the software. The simplest sentence type is a proposition stating a fact about the world, as in sentence 1. NL1 parses the sentence, translates the result into a TAL formula, and adds it to the knowledge base. Since the knowledge is expressed using logic we can define new relations in terms of old relations using axioms, as in the *support* relation of sentence 2. Before accepting new knowledge NL1 uses its reasoning capabilities to determine if the new information contradicts the current knowledge or if it

mrsToTal(MRS)
$R_{mrs} \leftarrow$ the list of relations in MRS
for each $r \in R_{mrs}$ do
  if r = the(x) or r = exists(x) then do $Q \leftarrow Q \cup \exists x$
  else if r = forall(x) then do $Q \leftarrow Q \cup \forall x$
  else if r = $rel(e_i, x_1, \ldots, x_n)$ then do
    $R_{tal} \leftarrow R_{tal} \cup$ [now] $rel(x_1, \ldots, x_n)$
  else if $r = rel(x)$ and rel is a background theory sort
    add $sort(x) = rel$ to the symbol table
  else do $R_{tal} \leftarrow R_{tal} \cup r$
return $q_1 \ldots q_i.[r_1 \wedge \ldots \wedge r_j]$
    where $q_1, \ldots, q_i \in Q$ and $r_1, \ldots, r_j \in R_{tal}$

Figure 4: The translation algorithm.

is already entailed and therefore redundant. That the table supports B1 is entailed by the previous fact and the axioms defining *support*, so the system simply replies yes. In sentence 3 we demonstrate the evaluation of a simple yes/no-question, although in this case the answer is not known since nothing has been said about block B2 and NL1 makes no closed world assumptions. Sentence 4 adds B2 to the table and B3 on top of B1 so that when the question in sentence 5 is evaluated it follows, from the fact that B3 is on B1 and the fact that a block cannot be in two places at the same time, that the table can not support B3. A much more complex type of questions is what-questions. Sentence 6 poses a what-question about another defined relation, *clear*. The system processes the question, as described in detail in Section 4, and constructs an answer MRS from which a complex natural language reply is generated. The sentences in 7 and 8 are recognized as imperative and are parsed into TAL action occurrences that are added to the world history. Finally, the question in sentence 9 demonstrates that the new blocksworld state conforms to the changes specified for the performed actions in the background action theory listed in Figure 7.

4 Sentence Processing

The sentence processing can be described by an (incomplete) algorithm, shown in figure 4, that translates a feature structure representation of an MRS into a TAL formula. To illustrate the algorithm let us assume that a user enters the question in Figure 5a. The LKB component parses the string and the MRS in Figure 5b is extracted from the resulting feature structure. The MRS Trans component uses the algorithm to interpret the sentence as a TAL formula, starting by con-

[2]http://www.franz.com/support/documentation/7.0/doc/prolog.html

a. "What blocks are on the table?"

b.
$$\begin{bmatrix} \text{predication} & \\ \text{mode} & \text{wh-ques} \\ \text{index} & e_1 \\ \text{liszt} & \left\langle \begin{matrix} \begin{bmatrix}\text{on} & \\ \text{ARG}_1 & e_1 \\ \text{ARG}_2 & x_1 \\ \text{ARG}_3 & x_2\end{bmatrix}, \begin{bmatrix}\text{table} & \\ \text{ARG}_1 & x_2\end{bmatrix}, \begin{bmatrix}\text{the} & \\ \text{ARG}_1 & x_2\end{bmatrix}, \\ \begin{bmatrix}\text{block} & \\ \text{ARG}_1 & x_1\end{bmatrix}, \begin{bmatrix}\text{exists} & \\ \text{ARG}_1 & x_1\end{bmatrix}, \begin{bmatrix}\text{answer} & \\ \text{ARG}_1 & x_1\end{bmatrix} \end{matrix} \right\rangle \end{bmatrix}$$

c.
```
(on e1 x1 x2) (table x2) (the x2)
(block x1) (exists x1) (answer x1)
```

d.
```
(exists (x2 x1)
  (and (on e1 x1 x2) (table x2)
       (block x1) (answer x1)))
```

e.
```
(exists (x2 x1)
  (and (time now (on x1 x2))
       (table x2) (block x1)
       (answer x1)))
```

f.
```
(exists (x2 x1)
  (and (time now (on x1 x2))
       (answer x1)))
```

$$sort(x1) = block, sort(x2) = table$$

Figure 5: Input processing for a question.

a.
```
(answer b2) (answer b1)
```

b.
```
(and
 (exists (x2) (time now (on b2 x2)))
 (exists (x4) (time now (on b1 x4))))
```

c.
```
(and e1 e2 e3)
(exists x2) (on e2 b2 x2)
(exists x4) (on e3 b1 x4)
```

d.
```
(and e1 e2 e3) (the x2) (on e2 x1 x2)
(b2 x1) (table x2) (the x4)
(on e3 x3 x4) (b1 x3) (table x4)
```

e.
$$\begin{bmatrix} \text{predication} & \\ \text{mode} & \text{prop} \\ \text{index} & e_1 \\ \text{liszt} & \left\langle \begin{matrix} \begin{bmatrix}\text{and} & \\ \text{ARG}_1 & e_1 \\ \text{ARG}_2 & e_2 \\ \text{ARG}_3 & e_3\end{bmatrix}, \begin{bmatrix}\text{on} & \\ \text{ARG}_1 & e_2 \\ \text{ARG}_2 & x_1 \\ \text{ARG}_3 & x_2\end{bmatrix}, \begin{bmatrix}\text{table} & \\ \text{ARG}_1 & x_2\end{bmatrix}, \\ \begin{bmatrix}\text{the} & \\ \text{ARG}_1 & x_2\end{bmatrix}, \begin{bmatrix}\text{b2} & \\ \text{ARG}_1 & x_1\end{bmatrix}, \begin{bmatrix}\text{on} & \\ \text{ARG}_1 & e_3 \\ \text{ARG}_2 & x_3 \\ \text{ARG}_3 & x_4\end{bmatrix}, \\ \begin{bmatrix}\text{table} & \\ \text{ARG}_1 & x_4\end{bmatrix}, \begin{bmatrix}\text{the} & \\ \text{ARG}_1 & x_4\end{bmatrix}, \begin{bmatrix}\text{b1} & \\ \text{ARG}_1 & x_3\end{bmatrix} \end{matrix} \right\rangle \end{bmatrix}$$

f. "B2 is on the table and B1 is on the table."

Figure 6: Answer processing and generation.

```
(domain block (b1 b2 b3))
(domain table (table1))
(domain surface (block table))
(fluent (holding block) boolean)
(fluent (on block surface) boolean)
(action (pickup block))
(action (putdown block surface))
(variable t time)
(variable block1 block)
(variable surface1 surface)
(variable surface2 surface)
(per (forall (t block1 surface1)
  (and (per t (holding block1))
       (per t (on block1 surface1)))))
(dep (forall (t block1 surface1 surface2)
  (-> (and (time t (on block1 surface1))
           (not (= surface1 surface2)))
   (time t (not (on block1 surface2))))))
(acs t1 t2 (pickup block1)
  (and (r (oc t1 t2) (holding block1))
    (forall (surface1)
      (r (oc t1 t2)
         (not (on block1 surface1))))))
(acs t1 t2 (putdown block1 surface1)
  (r (oc t1 t2)
     (and (not (holding block1))
          (on block1 surface1))))
(obs (forall (block1)
       (time 0 (not (holding block1)))))

(occ 0 1 (pickup b3))
(occ 1 2 (putdown b3 table1))
```

Figure 7: TAL representation of the blocksworld.

verting the MRS structure to a relation list, shown in Figure 5c. Our simple treatment of quantifiers assigns the scope of the entire formula while ordering each quantifier as they appear in the relation list and treating `the` as an existential quantifier, as in Figure 5d. In Figure 5e, the TAL time operator has been applied to create a temporal formula replacing the event variable `e1` with the designated constant `now` that is updated during the dialogue. Finally, to take advantage of the fact that TAL is an order-sorted logic, one-place relations that are identical to sorts defined in the current background theory are compiled into a symbol table and removed from the formula in Figure 5f.

At this point we have arrived at the TAL formula representing the user's question. Let us further assume that we are using the TAL blocksworld formalization shown in Figure 7, and that the current state of the dialogue interaction has produced the narrative history represented by the two final `occ` statements in the figure. These components together form a reasoning problem and any answer to the original question is an instantiation of the variable(s) selected by the special answer predicate in the question formula that satisfies the blocksworld specification together with the current world history.

Whatever method chosen, to solve the specific reasoning problem, will produce one or more answer formulas as show in Figure 6a. The answers are used to instantiate the question formula from Figure 5f to form the TAL representation in Figure 6b, representing the answers to the question. Again the MRS Trans module applies a number of processing steps, this time to construct an MRS structure representing the answers. First, the TAL time operator is translated into event variables and the quantifiers flattened to relations in Figure 6c. In Figure 6d, the references to the different blocks are made explicit in the relation list and the existential quantifier relations are translated to `the` relations, assuming the answer recipient knows what instance is meant. Finally, the MRS feature structure in Figure 6e is built and passed to the LKB module which uses the HPSG grammar to generate a natural language sentence corresponding to it. This sentence, displayed in Figure 6f, represents the natural language answer to the natural language question posed in Figure 5a.

5 Discussion

Natural language understanding was among the first research topics of artificial intelligence and has continued to be of great importance. As a consequence a large number of natural language understanding and dialogue systems have been built. Even though our system does not contribute any new techniques, it is a novel combination of existing techniques that form an environment in which a variety of linguistic and knowledge representation problems can be attacked.

Both the HPSG grammar and the TAL background knowledge are declarative knowledge sources that can be updated, incrementally and iteratively extended, or adapted to other use scenarios, independent of each other and most of the implementation components. They are also very expressive, contributing to the generality of the approach and to the goal of achieving representational adequacy. Equally important to expressiveness are issues of efficiency. Through a flexible compilation scheme for automated reasoning the tradeoff between expressiveness and efficiency is not set in stone but can be adapted to the task at hand. Different compilation steps can be implemented from different subsets of TAL to different automated reasoners and the choice of which compilation step to use is postponed.

While we have defended our design decisions we also acknowledge that they do give rise to some disadvantages. Relying on deep parsing might result in an instance of what is often called the "brittleness" problem where sentences slightly outside the competence of the grammar is totally incomprehensible and any grammatical error has similar results. We agree to some extent with this objection but note that there is interesting work on a Robust Minimal Recursion Semantics (Copestake, 2003) that would help integrate deep and shallow parsing. However, it should be pointed out that certain problems can never be solved using shallow methods and the mixing of deep and shallow methods can only obscure their solutions. Although generality was listed as an advantage, we also include it as a system drawback and possible point of attack by critics. A more general system will always be worse at any given task than a less general system that is more specialized toward that task. This rule weakens as the complexity of the task grows, but holds for most problems dealt with in current AI research.

5.1 Evaluation

Ultimately deciding on the viability of a framework such as NL1 should depend in some way on evaluation, but we have yet to perform any structured evaluation attempts and it is far from obvious how they would be implemented. The emphasis is not on the immediate improvement in the measurable efficiency of some real-world task like natural language translation, or the maximum coverage of a large number of question answering tasks, but instead on the investigation and exploration of a potentially fruitful marriage between natural language and knowledge representation technologies. At the same time, it is clear that there are obvious improvements that could be made to the current NL1 system, and that one would like to formulate some measure that made what is intuitively obvious, objectively evident. To this end we propose evaluations through a problem collection.

Even a very simple system can answer an infinite number of questions correctly if all that is varied is some trivial question property such as the name of the blocks in a blocksworld. It is not sufficient to count the number of sentences that are answered without further classifying them according to some complexity dimension, which is easier said than done. But even without this classification, one carefully selected sentence, illustrative of some complexity of language or reasoning, can still make or break a system. We propose that one creates and maintains an online collection of such examples, similar to the common-sense reasoning problem page (Morgenstern, 2005), the logically reasoning agents problem page (Thielscher, 2005), or the logic modelling workshop (Sandewall, 2005). New examples, illustrating new difficulties, would be submitted by different researchers and added to the problem page (with moderation). Evaluating different versions of the same system would then simply be accomplished by noting that the new version solves some additional question (ignoring, among others, issues of efficiency). Comparisons between systems would be entirely possible if one system subsumes the sentences correctly handled by the other system and possible with subjective results if the systems had a partial overlap.

5.2 Limitations and Future Work

We think this project has only scratched the surface of what is possible to accomplish using these techniques and that the proposed architecture has great potential. This section will point out the most important current limitations as well as our plans for continued development.

An obvious improvement is an extension of the HPSG grammar coverage to make the dialogue more varied and robust. The grammar does not at present even cover all the language constructs described in the book that it is based on (Sag et al., 2003) and there are certainly other HPSG grammar work that can be adapted to our system to further complement and extend coverage. An interesting experiment would be a coupling to the English resource grammar (Copestake and Flickinger, 2000).

Another extension that would put our approach to the test is a method of dealing with different forms of reference. We envision that, in addition to the domain background theory, the knowledge representation module will contain a model of the ongoing dialogue expressed using the same temporal action logic. Reference resolution would then be the solution of additional reasoning problems where objects that simultaneously fulfilled declarative constraints from dialogue factors, such as recency, and background knowledge, would be retrieved.

Time is a central concept in the system, yet at present this is not taken advantage of. Questions are all in present tense, even though everything is set up so as to support one talking to the system about past actions and time.

The current implementation recognizes commands of action and executes them, but such commands are restricted to simple atomic operations and the system can not by itself plan a sequence of actions in response to a user request. As part of another project, we are working on extending TAL to incorporate composite actions and action sequences or plans. Such work would fit naturally in the framework we have described here and would enable a seamless transition between requesting simple actions and requesting complex actions, possibly requiring the use of deductive planning, without extending the system architecture with a special purpose planner.

The compilation approach to automated TAL reasoning is inherently suitable for experimentation. While we have already performed work in this direction, developing several different compilations to first-order logic and another to logic programs, we do not expect to run out of ideas in this area. An especially interesting one is the use of deduction system alternatives to resolution, such as natural deduction, that might be more suitable for the kinds of inferences needed in the logicist approach to natural language understanding.

6 Related Work

An early and very impressive demonstration of natural language understanding was the SHRDLU system (Winograd, 1971). NL1 improves upon SHRDLU by using modern HPSG grammars instead of CFG grammars and declarative instead of procedural knowledge representation, but still falls short of the complexity of correctly executed dialogues. Though we are confident that our more general system architecture will catch up in the long run.

More recent work was carried out in the CLARE project (Alshawi et al., 1992) to provide natural language question answering interfaces for databases. The Core Language Engine parses questions into a quasi-logical form, aptly called QLF, that is interpreted and reasoned about in the context of background knowledge. In addition to the choice of parsing environment and intermediate form, two differences from NL1 are that we explicitly avoid committing to a specific reasoning paradigm while CLARE is based on the logic programming paradigm, and that the scale of the CLARE project is simply vastly larger than ours.

The idea of using other theorem proving techniques than logic programming to aid natural language understanding has also been explored previously. The work in (Blackburn et al., 1998) uses Dynamic Logic as the semantical representation and a translation to a fragment of first-order logic together with the Bliksem theorem prover as the reasoning mechanism. The feasibility of the set-up is demonstrated by using it to resolve discourse ambiguities. Our approach is similar in the application of an automated theorem prover after a translation step, but our background knowledge is encoded in Temporal Action Logic, which endows the system with the power to perform actions and reason about their effects.

Other systems, such as the architecture described in (Allen et al., 2001), deal with dialogues in realistic scenarios where human users want to interact with the system as fluently as possible to accomplish a task. Such efforts strive for *human-like* behaviour while we consider the ultimate goal to be *human-level*, but possibly very artificial, behaviour and hypothesize that many issues in human dialogues might well be ignored. Our interest lies not in modelling dialogue phenomena, but in using knowledge representation techniques for natural language understanding in a system with a dialogue interface.

Acknowledgements

We would like to thank Lars Ahrenberg for guidance and helpful discussions.

References

James Allen, George Ferguson, and Amanda Stent. 2001. An architecture for more realistic conversational systems. In *Proceedings of the 6th International Conference on Intelligent User Interfaces IUI'01*, pages 1–8. ACM Press.

Hiyan Alshawi, David Carter, Richard Crouch, Steve Pulman, Manny Rayner, and Arnold Smith. 1992. CLARE: A contextual reasoning and cooperative response framework for the core language engine. Technical Report CRC-028, SRI International.

Patrick Blackburn, Johan Bos, Michael Kohlhase, and Hans de Nivelle. 1998. Automated theorem proving for natural language understanding. In *Problem-solving Methodologies with Automated Deduction (Workshop at CADE-15)*.

Ann Copestake and Dan Flickinger. 2000. An open-source grammar development environment and broad-coverage english grammar using HPSG. In *Proceedings of the Second Conference on Language Resources and Evaluation LREC-2000*.

Ann Copestake. 2003. Report on the design of RMRS. Technical Report D1.1a, University of Cambridge.

Patrick Doherty and Witold Łukaszewicz. 1994. Circumscribing features and fluents. In *Proceedings of the 1st International Conference on Temporal Logic ICTL'94*, volume 827 of *Lecture Notes in AI*, pages 82–100. Springer.

Patrick Doherty, Joakim Gustafsson, Lars Karlsson, and Jonas Kvarnström. 1998. Temporal action logics (TAL): Language specification and tutorial. *Linköping Electronic Articles in Computer and Information Science*, 3(15).

Patrick Doherty. 1994. Reasoning about action and change using occlusion. In *Proceedings of the Eleventh European Conference on Artificial Intelligence ECAI'94*, pages 401–405. John Wiley and Sons.

Vladimir Lifschitz, 1994. *Circumscription*, volume 3 of *Handbook of Logic in Artificial Intelligence and Logic Programming*, chapter 6, pages 298–352. Oxford University Press.

Leora Morgenstern. 2005. The common-sense reasoning problem page. `http://www-formal.stanford.edu/leora/commonsense/`. Visited February 2006.

Ivan A. Sag, Thomas Wasow, and Emily M. Bender. 2003. *Syntactic Theory: A Formal Introduction (Second Edition)*. CSLI Publications.

Erik Sandewall. 1994. *Features and Fluents: The Representation of Knowledge about Dynamical Systems*, volume 1. Oxford University Press.

Erik Sandewall. 2005. Logic modelling workshop. `http://www.ida.liu.se/ext/etai/lmw/`. Visited December 2005.

Mark E. Stickel. 2005. SNARK - SRI's new automated reasoning kit. `http://www.ai.sri.com/~stickel/snark.html`. Visited December 2005.

Michael Thielscher. 2005. Logically reasoning agents problem page. `http://www.cl.inf.tu-dresden.de/~mit/LRAPP/`. Visited December 2005.

Terry Winograd. 1971. Procedures as a representation for data in a computer program for understanding natural language. Technical Report 235, MIT Artificial Intelligence Laboratory.

Merging Stories with Shallow Semantics

Fiona McNeill
School of Informatics
Univ. of Edinburgh
f.j.mcneill@ed.ac.uk

Harry Halpin
School of Informatics
Univ. of Edinburgh
h.halpin@ed.ac.uk

Ewan Klein
School of Informatics
Univ. of Edinburgh
ewan@inf.ed.ac.uk

Alan Bundy
School of Informatics
Univ. of Edinburgh
bundy@inf.ed.ac.uk

Abstract

We demonstrate a proof-of-concept system that uses a shallow chunking-based technique for knowledge extraction from natural language text, in particular looking at the task of story understanding. This technique is extended with a reasoning engine that borrows techniques from dynamic ontology refinement to discover the semantic similarity of stories and to merge them together.

1 Introduction

Many NLP applications would benefit from the availability of broad-coverage knowledge extraction from natural language text. Despite some recent advances in this direction (Bos et al., 2004), it is still the case that it is hard to obtain deep semantic analyses which are accurate enough to support logical inference (Lev et al., 2004).

Our problem can be stated in abstract terms. Given a formalism F for the semantic representation of natural language, such as first-order clauses in predicate calculus, and a set of sentences S, give a translation function $T(S) \rightarrow F$. The goal of such a translation would be to solve a problem P (such as paraphrasing or question-answering) where F allows P to be solved by some reasoning process, or else the domain exhibits a type of structure easily represented in the formalism F.

If we accept that current parsing technology cannot reliably combine accurate semantic analysis with robustness, then the question arises whether 'noisy' semantics can be ameliorated using some other techniques. In this paper, we adopt the hypothesis that methods drawn from dynamic ontology refinement (McNeill et al., 2004) can indeed help with this task. In the limit, we would like to be able to show that semantic content drawn from a wide variety of sources can be compared and merged to reveal the shared common ground. However, in this paper we have limited ourselves to a much more modest goal, namely merging and comparing semantic content from a set of variants of a single story.[1]

We obtained the variants by asking adults to retell the story, based on hearing the original, or reading it themselves. We have developed a system that can take in any number of such stories and produce a merged version of the stories. Our re-tellers were instructed not to elaborate upon or intentionally change the original and consequently the stories are fairly similar, not just in meaning but to an extent also in wording.

In the next two sections, we will first describe how semantic clauses are extracted from text, and second, how clauses obtained from different texts are merged.

2 Extracting Clauses from Text

The method we have adopted for extracting first-order clauses from text can be called 'semantic chunking.' This seems an appropriate term for two reasons. First, we use a syntactic chunker to identify noun groups and verb groups (i.e. non-recursive clusters of related words with a noun or verb head respectively). Second, we use a cascade of finite state rules to map from this shallow syntactic structure into first-order clauses; this cascade is conceptually very similar to the chunking method pioneered by Abney's Cass chunker (Abney, 1996).

The text processing framework we have used draws heavily on a suite of XML tools developed

[1] We used a simplifi ed version of Oscar Wilde's fairy story *The Selfish Giant*.

for generic XML manipulation (LTXML (Thompson et al., 1997)) as well as NLP-specific XML tools (LT-TTT (Grover et al., 2000), LT-CHUNK (Finch and Mikheev, 1997)). More recently, significantly improved upgrades of these tools have been developed, most notably the program *lxtransduce*, which performs rule-based transductions of XML structures. We have used *lxtransduce* both for the syntactic chunking (based on rule developed by Grover) and for construction of semantic clauses.

The main steps in the processing pipeline are as follows:

1. Words and sentences are tokenized.
2. The words are tagged for their part of speech using the CandC tagger (Clark and Curran, 2004) and the Penn Treebank tagset.
3. Pronoun resolution is carried out using the Glencova Pronoun Resolution algorithm (Halpin et al., 2004), based on a series of rules similar to the CogNIAC engine (Baldwin, 1997), but without gender information-based rules since this is not provided by the Penn Treebank tagset.
4. The words are then reduced to their morphological stem (lemma) using Morpha (Minnen et al., 2001).
5. The *lxtransduce* program is used to chunk the sentence into verb groups and noun groups.
6. In an optional step, words are tagged as Named Entities, using the CandC tagger trained on MUC data.
7. The partially chunked sentences are selectively mapped into semantic clauses in a series of steps, described in more detail below.
8. The XML representation of the clauses is converted using an XSLT stylesheet into a more conventional syntactic format for use by Prolog or other logic-based systems.

The output of the syntactic processing is an XML file containing word elements which are heavily annotated with attributes. Following CoNLL BIO notation (Tjong et al., 2000), chunk information is recorded at the word level. Heads of noun groups and verb groups are assigned semantic tags such as `arg` and `rel` respectively. In addition, other semantically relevant forms such as conjunction, negation, and prepositions are also tagged. Most other input and syntactic information is discarded at this stage. However, we maintain a record through shared indices of which terms belong to the same chunks. This is used, for instance, to build coordinated arguments.

Regular expressions over the semantically tagged elements are used to compose clauses, using the heuristic that an `arg` immediately preceding a `pred` is the subject of the clause, while `args` following the `pred` are complements. Since the heads of verb groups are annotated for voice, we can treat passive clauses appropriately, yielding a representation that is equivalent to the active congener. We also implement simple heuristics that allow us to capture simple cases of control and verb phrase ellipsis in many cases.

3 Knowledge Refinement and Merging

Once the clauses have been extracted from the text, each story becomes a list of predicates, representing verbs, each with a number of arguments (possibly zero), representing nouns. Two stories can thus be compared by considering how the clauses from one story relate to the clauses from another story. This is done both by considering how the predicates (verbs) from one story relate to those from another story and also by considering the arguments (nouns) that these related predicates connect. This allows us to consider not just the similarity of the words used in the story but also, to some extent, the structure of the sentences.

The aim of merging is to build up, initially, a *working merged story* that includes all aspects of each story so far; then, when all stories have been merged, to refine the working merged story by removing aspects of it that are considered to be peripheral to the main core. The output is a single story in the same format as the inputs, and which reflects common elements from across the set of variants.

If text is represented in such clause form, then the number of ways in which these clausal representations of the story can differ is strictly limited. Clauses have only two attributes: predicates and arguments. The predicates may find an exact match, an inexact match or no match. If the predicates find some kind of match, their arguments can then be examined. Each of these will find an exact, inexact, or no match with the corresponding argument in the related predicate; additionally, their ordering and number may be different. Thus it is possible to create an exhaustive list of the possible differences between clauses. We currently consider only WordNet information concerning synonyms, hypernyms and hyponyms when determining matches: we do not perform inference using antonyms, for example, nor do we consider implication cases.

The techniques that are used in the merging process were inspired by work on dynamic ontology refinement (McNeill et al., 2004), which deals with the problem of reasoning failure caused by small inconsistencies between largely similar ontologies. This is achieved by analysing ontological objects that were expected to, but do not, match, and diagnosing and patching these mismatches through consideration of how they differ through reasoning. Examples of mismatches that are common between similar ontologies are changed names of predicates (often to sub- or super-types), changed arity, and changed types of arguments. These types of ontological mismatches are currently handled by our system, since in the domain of stories people often use different names or different levels of description for things. The application of these techniques for determining differences and similarities between the story representations therefore forms the basis of the merging process.

In order to merge a new story with the current working merged story (WMS), the facts in the WMS are examined one by one in an attempt to match them to a fact in the story to be merged. Such a match may be exact (the predicates and all their arguments are identical), inexact (the predicates have the same name but their arguments differ), similar (the predicates are synonyms) or related (the predicates are hyponyms or hypernyms). Information about synonyms, hyponyms and hypernyms is extracted from WordNet and used as the type hierarchy for our refinement (see Section 5; for an explanation of our usage of WordNet, see the WordNet project (Miller, 1995) for general details). Another potential kind of match is where the arguments match but no link can be found between the predicates; however, this is not considered in the current system. If a match of any kind is found for a predicate from the WMS, the predicate from the new story with which it matches is appended to its entry in the WMS. Each entry in the WMS is annotated with a score to indicate in how many stories a match of some kind has been found for it. For example, an entry in the WMS, `([1] play(child))` may find an inexact match with `cavort(child)` in a new story, to create an entry of `([2] play(child), cavort(child))` in the new WMS.

Once all the facts in the WMS have been examined and matched where possible, there will usually be some facts in the story to be merged that have not been found as a match for anything in the WMS. These should not be ignored; they have no match with anything thus far, but it may be that stories to be merged in future will find a match with them. Thus, they are added to the merged story with a score of 1. The initial merged story is found by simply annotating the first story to be merged so that each entry has a score of 1. It is possible, but not necessary, to provide a range value to the merging process, so that matches are only sought in the given vicinity of the fact in the WMS. If no range value is given, this is set to be arbitrarily large so that all of the story to be merged is examined.

Once all of the stories to be merged have been examined, we have a complete WMS, which needs to be processed to produce the merged output. A threshold value is used to determine which of these should be immediately discarded: anything with a score less than the threshold. Those with a score of more than or equal to the threshold must be processed so that each is represented by a single fact, rather than a list of different versions of the fact. If all versions of the fact are identical, this single version is the output. Otherwise, both a 'canonical' name and 'canonical' arguments for a fact must be calculated. In the current system, a simple approach is taken to this. For the predicate, if there is more than one version, then the most commonly occurring one is chosen as the canonical representative. If there are two or more that are jointly the most commonly occurring, then the most specific of the names is chosen (i.e., the one that is lowest in the class hierarchy). When choosing the arguments for the merged predicate, any argument that has a match in at least one other version of the predicate is included. If the match is inexact — i.e., the arguments are not of the same class, but are of related classes — then the most specific of the classes is chosen.

4 Worked Example

We now work through a simplified example to illustrate the merging process. Consider the following three lists of facts, which are drawn from different retellings of our example story:

Story 1: `come(child), play(garden), visit(friend), forget(friend), come(giant), yell(child)`

Story 2: `go(giant), visit(friend), be(giant), come(child), play(garden)`

Story 3: `be(giant), come(giant), play(garden), bellow(child,anger,giant), happy(giant)`

The first WMS (working merged story) is produced by marking up the first story:

```
([1] come(child)),
([1] play(garden)),
([1] visit(friend)),
([1] forget(friend)),
([1] come(giant)),
([1] yell(child))
```

This is then merged with the second story. The first fact of Story 1, `come(child)`, matches exactly with the fourth fact of the Story 2; the fifth fact matches inexactly with the fourth fact of the Story 2, and so on. The resulting WMS is:

```
([2] come(child), come(child)),
([2] play(garden), play(garden)),
([2] visit(friend) visit(friend)),
([1] forget(friend)),
([1] come(giant)),
([1] yell(child)),
([1] come(giant)),
([1] go(giant)),
([1] be(giant))
```

This is then merged with Story 3 to produce:

```
([3] come(child), come(child),
    come(giant)),
([3] play(garden), play(garden),
    play(garden)),
([2] visit(friend) visit(friend)),
([1] forget(friend)),
([1] come(giant)),
([2] yell(child),
    bellow(child,anger,giant)),
([1] come(giant)),
([1] go(giant)),
([2] be(giant), be(giant)),
([1] happy(giant))
```

We then proceed to merge all the automatically extracted knowledge representations of the three stories. To create the output merged story, those predicates with a score of 1 are ignored. The others are each merged to produce a single predicate. For example, `([3] come(child), come(child), come(giant))` becomes `come(child)`: `giant` does not match with any other argument and is dropped. `([2] yell(child), bellow(child,anger,giant))` becomes `yell(child)` because `yell` is a subclass of `bellow`, and thus preferred, and `child` is the only argument that has a match in both facts. Thus the resulting merged story is:

```
come(child),
play(garden),
visit(friend),
yell(child),
be(giant)
```

It is clear from this example that our current approach is, at times, naive. For example, the decisions about which arguments to include in output facts, and how to order facts that are unmatched in working merged stories could be made significantly more effective. We view this current system as a proof of concept that such an approach can be useful; we certainly do not consider the system to be complete approach to the problem. Further work on the system would result in improved performance.

5 Extracting Ontological Information from WordNet

In order to perform some of the tasks involved in merging and matching, it is necessary to have information about how words are related. We extract this information from WordNet by getting the ontology refinement engine to call WordNet with a word and retrieve both its synset (i.e., synomym set) and its hyponyms and hypernyms. We collect these for every sense of the word, since our natural language pipeline currently does not include word-sense disambiguation. When it is necessary during the merging process to obtain information about whether two words are related (i.e., when two words do not match exactly), we extract synonym and hyper/hyponym information from WordNet for these words and examine it to discover whether an exact match exists or not. We treat synonyms as equivalent, and we treat hypernym and hyponym synsets as the super- and subtype of a word respectively, and then traverse the type hierarchy for exact matches. To avoid spurious equivalence we use a bound to restrict the search, and from our experience a bound of two type-levels in either direction and a stop-list of 'upper ontology' types yields good results.

6 Related Work

This work breaks some new ground by being the first to use dynamic refinement to compare and merge information from natural language texts. In general, recent work in natural language processing has currently relied heavily on 'purely statistical' methods for tasks such as text similarity and summarization. However, there is also a rich logical tradition in linguistic semantics, and work in this vein can bring the two closer together.

Current work in story understanding is focusing on the use of logical forms, yet these are not extracted from text automatically (Mueller, 2003). The natural language processing and story conversion pipeline are improvements over a pipeline that was shown to successfully compare stories in a manner similar to a teacher (Halpin et al., 2004).

The merging task is a more logic-based approach than similar techniques like information fusion used in multi-document summarization (Barzilay et al., 1999). Our approach has some features in common with (Wan and Dale, 2001), however, we have chosen to focus exclusively on merger at the semantic level, rather than trying to also incorporate syntactic structure.

There has also been a revival in using weighted logical forms in structured relational learning, such as Markov Logic Networks (Domingos and Kok, 2005), and this is related to the scoring of facts used by the current system in merging texts. As mentioned at the beginning of this paper, the conversion of unrestricted text to some logical form has experienced a recent revival recently (Bos et al., 2004). Although our approach deliberately ignores much semantic detail, this may be compensated for by increased robustness due to the reliance on finite-state methods for semantic translation and chunking.

7 Further Work

The work we have done thus far suggests many avenues for further work. One obvious improvement would be to enable the system to deal with more complex input, so that stories could be represented with nested predicates and with a more complex notion of time. Time can be conceived of ontologically in a number of differing manners with highly differing properties, and relating these notions of time to the extraction of tense (which the *lxtransduce*-based chunker currently does automatically) would be a fruitful task (Hayes, 1996). Making decisions about what to include in a merged story is currently done in a fairly naive manner. Further research into what constituted a good merged story and under what circumstances it is advantageous to be sceptical or generous as to what should be included in the merged story, would allow this to become much more effective. Once the system has been suitably improved, it should be tested on a more complex domain, such as news stories. Finally, the primary benefit of the use of knowledge representation is the possibility of using inference. The current system could easily take advantage of an external knowledge-base of domain-specific facts and rules to aid refinement and merging.

We have not implemented a baseline for the system using purely word-based statistical features, such as reducing the words to the their morphological stem and then using WordNet synsets to compare the stories without any predicate structure. This is because at this stage in development the extraction of the correct clauses is itself the goal of the task. If connected to larger system, comparison with a purely statistical model would be useful. However, we would hazard a guess that in the domain of computational story understanding, it is unlikely that purely statistical methods would work well, since stories by their nature consist of events involving the actions of characters in a particular temporal order, and this type of structural complexity would seem to be best accounted for by some structure-preserving features that attempt to model and extract these events explicitly.

8 Conclusion

Although many questions remain unanswered, the development of the current system demonstrates that this kind of refinement-based approach to matching and merging texts can be produce promising results. Much could be done to improve the effectiveness of both the clause extraction and the merging components of the system, and the breadth of task that these techniques have been tested on remains very narrow. Nevertheless, this work represents a reasonably successful first investigation of the problem, and we intend to use it as the basis for further work.

References

Steven Abney. 1996. Partial parsing via finite-state cascades. *Natural Language Engineering*, 2(4):337–344.

Breck Baldwin. 1997. CogNIAC: A High Precision Pronoun Resolution Engine. In *Operational Factors in Practical, Robust Anaphora Resolution for Unrestricted Texts (ACL-97 workshop)*, pages 38–45.

R. Barzilay, K. McKeown, and M. Elhadad. 1999. Information fusion in the context of multi-document summarization. In *In Proceedings of Association for*

Computational Linguistics, pages 550–557, Maryland.

Johan Bos, Stephen Clark, Mark Steedman, James Curran, and Julia Hockenmaier. 2004. Wide-coverage semantic representations from a CCG parser. In *In Proceedings of the 20th International Conference on Computational Linguistics (COLING '04)*, pages 1240–1246, Geneva, Switzerland.

Stephen Clark and James Curran. 2004. Parsing the WSJ using CCG and log-linear models. In *Proceedings of the 42nd Annual Meeting of the Association for Computational Linguistics (ACL 2004)*, pages 104–111, Barcelona, Spain.

Pedro Domingos and Stanley Kok. 2005. Learning the structure of Markov Logic Networks. In *Proceedings of the International Conference on Machine Learning*, pages 441–448, Bonn.

Steve Finch and Andrei Mikheev. 1997. A workbench for finding structure in texts. In Walter Daelemans and Miles Osborne, editors, *Proceedings of the Fifth Conference on Applied Natural Language Processing (ANLP-97)*. Washington D.C.

Claire Grover, Colin Matheson, Andrei Mikheev, and Marc Moens. 2000. LT TTT—a flexible tokenisation tool. In *LREC 2000—Proceedings of the 2nd International Conference on Language Resources and Evaluation*, pages 1147–1154.

Harry Halpin, Johanna Moore, and Judy Robertson. 2004. Automatic analysis of plot for story rewriting. In *Proceedings of Empirical Methods in Natural Language Processing*, pages 127–133, Barcelona, Spain.

Pat Hayes. 1996. A catalog of temporal theories. Technical Report UIUC-BI-AI-96-01, University of Illinois.

Iddo Lev, Bill MacCartney, Christopher D. Manning, and Roger Levy. 2004. Solving logic puzzles: From robust processing to precise semantics. In *2nd Workshop on Text Meaning and Interpretation at ACL 2004*, pages 9–16.

Fiona McNeill, Alan Bundy, and Chris Walton. 2004. Facilitating agent communication through detecting, diagnosing and refining ontological mismatch. In *Proceedings of the KR2004 Doctoral Consortium*. AAAI Technical Report.

George Miller. 1995. Wordnet: A lexical database for english. *Communications of the ACM*, 11(38):39–41.

Guido Minnen, John Carroll, and David Pearce. 2001. Applied morphological processing of English. *Natural Language Engineering*, 7(3):207–203.

Erik T. Mueller. 2003. Story understanding through multi-representation model construction. In Graeme Hirst and Sergei Nirenburg, editors, *Text Meaning: Proceedings of the HLT-NAACL 2003 Workshop*, pages 46–53, East Stroudsburg, PA. Association for Computational Linguistics.

Henry Thompson, Richard Tobin, David McKelvie, and Chris Brew. 1997. LT XML: Software API and toolkit for XML processing.

Erik F. Tjong, Kim Sang, and Sabine Buchholz. 2000. Introduction to the CoNLL-2000 shared task: Chunking. In *Proceedings of the Conference on Natural Language Learning (CoNLL-2000)*. Lisbon, Portugal.

Stephen Wan and Robert Dale. 2001. Merging sentences using shallow semantic analysis: A first experiment. In *Proceedings of the 2001 Australasian Natural Language Processing Workshop*, Sydney, April. Macquarie University.

Numerical Data Integration for Cooperative Question-Answering

Véronique Moriceau
Institut de Recherche en Informatique de Toulouse
118, route de Narbonne
31062 Toulouse cedex 09, France
moriceau@irit.fr

Abstract

In this paper, we present an approach which aims at providing numerical answers in a question-answering system. These answers are generated in a cooperative way: they explain the variation of numerical values when several values, apparently incoherent, are extracted from the web as possible answers to a question.

1 Introduction

Search engines on the web and most existing question-answering systems provide the user with a set of hyperlinks and/or web page extracts containing answer(s) to a question. These answers may be incoherent to a certain degree: they may be equivalent, complementary, contradictory, at different levels of precision or specifity, etc. It is then quite difficult for the user to know which answer is the correct one.

In a cooperative perspective, we propose an approach for answer generation in natural language which uses answer **integration**. When several possible answers are selected by the extraction engine, the goal is to define a coherent core from candidate answers and to generate a **cooperative answer**, i.e. an answer with explanations. We assume that all web pages are equally reliable since page *provenance* information (defined in (McGuinness and Pinheiro da Silva, 2004) e.g., source, date, author, etc.) is difficult to obtain.

To adequately deal with data integration in question-answering, it is essential to define precisely relations existing between potential answers. In this introduction, we first present related works. Then, we define a general typology of relations between candidate answers.

1.1 Related works

Most of existing systems on the web produce a set of answers to a question in the form of hyperlinks or page extracts, ranked according to a relevance score. For example, COGEX (Moldovan et al., 2003) uses its logic prover to extract lexical relationships between the question and its candidate answers. The answers are then ranked based on their proof scores. Other systems define relationships between web page extracts or texts containing possible answers: for example, (Radev and McKeown, 1998) and (Harabagiu and Lacatusu, 2004) define *agreement* (when two sources report the same information), *addition* (when a second source reports additional information), *contradiction* (when two sources report conflicting information), etc. These relations can be classified into the 4 relations defined by (Webber et al., 2002), i.e. **inclusion**, **equivalence**, **aggregation** and **alternative** which we present below.

Most question-answering systems provide answers which take into account neither information given by all candidate answers nor their inconsistency. This is the point we focus on in the following section.

1.2 A general typology of integration mechanisms

To better characterize our problem, we collected a corpus of about 100 question-answer pairs in French that reflect different inconsistency problems (most of pairs are obtained via Google or QRISTAL[1]). We first assume that all candidate answers obtained via an extraction engine are potentially correct, i.e. they are of the semantic type expected by the question.

[1] www.qristal.fr, Synapse Développement.

For each question of our corpus, a set of possible answers is extracted from the web. The goal of our corpus analysis is to identify relations between those answers and to define a general typology of associated integration mechanisms. We use for this purpose the 4 relations defined in (Webber et al., 2002) and for each relation, we propose one or several integration mechanisms in order to generate answers which take into account characteristics and particularities of candidate answers.

1.2.1 Inclusion

A candidate answer is in an inclusion relation if it entails another answer (for example, concepts of candidate answers linked in an ontology by the *is-a* or *part-of* relations). For example, *in Brittany* and *in France* are correct answers to the question *Where is Brest?*, linked by an inclusion relation since *Brittany* is a part of *France*.

1.2.2 Equivalence

Candidate answers which are linked by an equivalence relation are consistent and entail mutually. The corpus analysis allows us to identify two main types of equivalence:

(1) Lexical equivalence: use of acronyms or foreign language, synonymies, metonymies, paraphrases, proportional series. For example, to the question *Who killed John Lennon?*, *Mark Chapman, the murderer of John Lennon* and *John Lennon's killer Mark Chapman* are equivalent answers.

(2) Equivalence with inference: in a number of cases, some common knowledge, inferences or computations are necessary to detect equivalence relations. For example, *The A320 is 22* and *The A320 was built in 1984* are equivalent answers to the question *How old is the Airbus A320?*.

1.2.3 Aggregation

The aggregation relation defines a set of consistent answers when the question accepts several different ones. In this case, all candidate answers are potentially correct and can be integrated in the form of a conjunction of all these answers. For example, an answer to the question *Where is Disneyland?* can be *in Tokyo, Paris, Hong-Kong and Los Angeles*.

1.2.4 Alternative

The alternative relation defines a set of inconsistent answers. In the case of questions expecting a unique answer, only one answer among candidates is correct. On the contrary, all candidates can be correct answers.

(1) A simple solution is to propose a disjunction of candidate answers. For example, if the question *When does autumn begin?* has the candidate answers *Autumn begins on September 21st* and *Autumn begins on September 20th*, an answer such as *Autumn begins on either September 20th or September 21st* can be proposed. (Moriceau, 2005) proposes an integration method for answers of type *date*.

(2) If candidate answers have common characteristics, it is possible to integrate them according to these characteristics ("greatest common denominator"). For example, the question *When does the "fête de la musique" take place?* has the following answers *June 1st 1982, June 21st 1983, ..., June 21st 2005*. Here, the extraction engine selects pages containing the dates of music festivals over the years. Since these candidate answers have day and month in common, an answer such as *The "fête de la musique" takes place every June 21st* can be proposed (Moriceau, 2005).

(3) Numerical values can be integrated in the form of an interval, average or comparison. For example, if the question *How far is Paris from Toulouse?* has the candidate answers *713 km, 678 km* and *681 km*, answers such as *Paris is at about 690 km from Toulouse* (average) or *The distance between Paris and Toulouse is between 678 and 713 km* (interval) can be proposed.

2 Motivations

In this paper, we focus on answer elaboration from several answers of type *numerical* (case (3) above). Numerical questions deal with numerical properties such as distance, quantity, weight, age, etc. In order to identify the different problems, let us consider the following example :
What is the average age of marriage in France?
- In 1972, the average age of marriage was 24.5 for men and 22.4 for women. In 2005, it is 30 for men and 28 for women.
- According to an investigation carried out by FNAIM in 1999, the average age of marriage is 27.7 for women and 28.9 for men.
- The average age of marriage in France increased from 24.5 to 26.9 for women and from 26.5 to 29 for men between 1986 and 1995.

This set of potential answers may seem incoherent but their internal coherence can be made ap-

parent once a variation criterion is identified. In a cooperative perspective, an answer can be for example:
In 2005, the average age of marriage in France is 30 for men and 28 for women.
It increased by about 5.5 years between 1972 and 2005.
This answer is composed of:

1. a direct answer to the question,
2. an explanation characterizing the variation mode of the numerical value.

To generate this kind of answer, it is necessary (1) to integrate candidate answers in order to elaborate a direct answer (for example by solving inconsistencies), and (2) to integrate candidate answers characteristics in order to generate an explanation.

In the following sections, we first define a typology of numerical answers and then briefly present the general architecture of the system which generates cooperative numerical answers.

2.1 A typology of numerical answers

To define the different types of numerical answers, we collected a set of 80 question-answer pairs about prices, quantities, age, time, weight, temperature, speed and distance. The goal is to identify for each question-answer pair:
- if the question expects one or several answers (learnt from texts and candidate answers),
- why extracted numerical values are different (is this an inconsistency? an evolution?).

2.1.1 The question accepts only one answer

For example, *How long is the Cannes International Film Festival?*. In this case, if there are several candidate answers, there is an inconsistency which has to be solved (cf. section 4.1).

2.1.2 The question accepts several answers

This is the case when numerical values vary according to certain criteria. Let us consider the following examples.

Example 1 :
How many inhabitants are there in France?
- Population census in France (1999): 61632485.
- 61.7: number of inhabitants in France in 2004.
In this example, the numerical value (quantity) is a property which changes over time (*1999*, *2004*).

Example 2 :
What is the average age of marriage of women in 2004?
- In Iran, the average age of marriage of women went from 19 to 21 years in 2004.
- In 2004, Moroccan women get married at the age of 27.
In this example, the numerical value (age of marriage) varies according to place (*in Iran*, *Moroccan*).

Example 3 :
At which temperature do I have to serve wine?
- Red wine must be served at room temperature.
- Champagne: between 8 and 10 °C.
- White wine: between 8 and 11 °C.
Here, the numerical value (temperature) varies according to the question focus (wine).

The corpus analysis allows us to identify 3 main variation criteria, namely *time, place* and *restriction* (restriction on the focus, for example: Champagne/wine). These criteria can be combined: some numerical values vary according to time and place, to time and restrictions, etc. (for example, the average age of marriage vary according to time, place and restrictions on men/women). Note that there are several levels of restrictions and that only restrictions of the same type can be compared (cf. section 3.2). For example, *metropolitan population* and *population of overseas regions* are restrictions of the same ontological type (geographical place) whereas *prison population* is a restriction of a different type and is not comparable to the previous ones.

2.2 Architecture of the system

Figure 1 presents the general architecture of our system which allows us to generate answers and explanations from several different numerical answers.

Questions are submitted in natural language to QRISTAL which analyses them (focus, answer expected type) and which selects potential answers from the web: QRISTAL searches web pages containing the keywords of the query and synonyms (extraction engine). Then, an extraction grammar constructs a set of frames from candidate web pages. From the frame set, the variation criteria and mode of the searched numerical value are identified. Finally, a natural language answer is generated explaining those characteristics. Each of these stages is presented in the next sections.

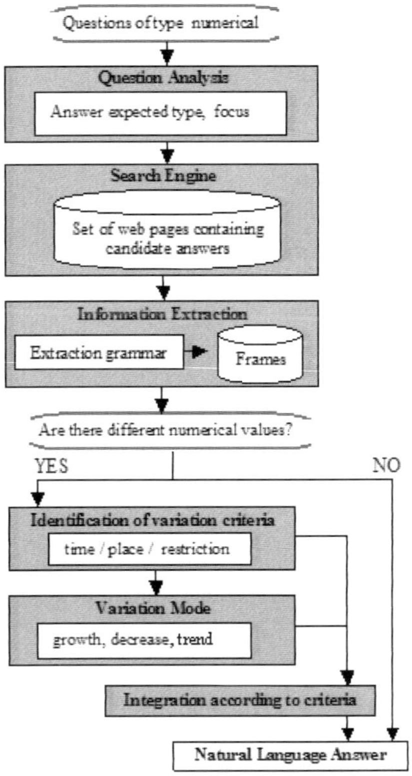

Figure 1: Architecture

3 Answer characterization

Answer characterization consists in 2 main stages:
- information extraction from candidate web pages,
- characterization of variation (criteria and mode) of numerical values if necessary.

3.1 Answer extraction

Once QRISTAL has selected candidate web pages (those containing the question focus and having the expected semantic type), a grammar is applied to extract information needed for the generation of an appropriate cooperative answer. This information is mainly:
- the searched numerical value (*val*),
- the *unit* of measure,
- the question focus and its synonyms (*focus*) (for the moment, synonyms are not considered because it requires a lot of resources, especially in an open domain),
- the *date* and *place* of the information,
- the *restriction(s)* on the question focus (essentially, adjectives or relative clauses).

In addition, the corpus analysis shows that some other information is essential for infering the precision degree or the variation mode of values. It is mainly linguistic clues indicating:
- the *precision* of the numerical value (for example adverbs or prepositions such as in *about 700, ...*),
- a *variation* of the value (for example temporal adverbs, verbs of change/movement as in *the price* **increased** *to 200 euro*).

We define a frame a_i which gathers all this information for a numerical value:

$$a_i = \begin{bmatrix} Val = \\ Precision = \\ Unit = \\ Focus = \\ Date = \\ Place = \\ Restriction = \\ Variation = \end{bmatrix}$$

A dedicated grammar extracts this information from candidate web pages and produces the set A of N candidate answers: $A = \{a_1, ..., a_N\}$. We use a gapping grammar (Dahl and Abramson, 1984) to gap elements which are not useful (in the example **According to an investigation carried out by FNAIM** *in 1999, the average age of marriage is 27.7 for women and 28.9 for men*, elements in bold are not useful). We give below the main rules of the grammar, optional elements are between brackets:

Answer → Nominal Sentence | Verbal Sentence
Nominal Sentence → Focus (Restriction), ..., (Date), ..., (Place), ..., (Precision) Val (Unit)
Verbal Sentence → Focus (Restriction), ..., (Date), ..., (Place), ..., Verb, ..., (Precision) Val (Unit)
Verb → VerbQuestion | Variation
VerbQuestion → *count* | *estimate* | *weigh* | ...
Variation → *go up* | *decrease* | ...
Precision → *about* | *on average* | ...
Place → Country | City | ...
Time → Date | Period | ...
Restriction → Adjective | Relative | ...
....

Figure 2 shows an extraction result.

A syntactic analysis is also necessary to check the relevance of extracted information. For example, suppose that the answer *population of cities of France which have more than 2000 inhabitants (...)* is proposed to the question *How many inhabitants are there in France?*. A syntactic analysis has to identify the expression *cities of France which (...)* as a restriction of *population* and to

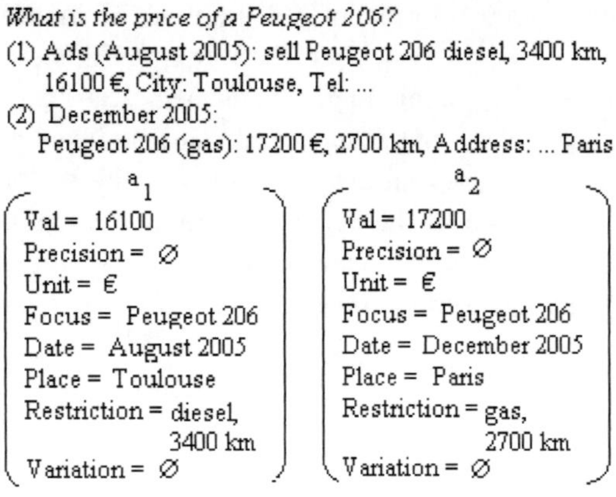

Figure 2: Results of extraction

infer that *2000 inhabitants* is a property of those cities and that it is not an answer to the question. We plan to investigate the lexical elements (prepositions, predicative terms, etc.) necessary to this analysis.

Elements of extraction evaluation are presented in figure 3: we submitted 30 questions to Google and QRISTAL. Our system can select the correct direct answer provided that QRISTAL returns the correct answer among relevant pages (for 87% of the questions we evaluated) and that our grammar succeeds in extracting relevant information (this has to be evaluated).

Google		
Correct Answer's Rank (average)	Incorrect Answer before the correct one	Relevant Pages (first 30 links)
4	43%	23%
QRISTAL		
Correct Answer	Correct Answer among relevant pages	Relevant Pages (first 30 links)
13%	87%	30%

Figure 3: Elements of evaluation

3.2 Variation criteria

Once we have the frames representing the different numerical values, the goal is to determine if there is a variation and to identify the variation criteria of the value. In fact, we assume that there is a variation if there is at least k different numerical values with different criteria (time, place, restriction) among the N frames (k is a rate which depends on N: the more candidate answers there are, the greater is k). Thus, a numerical value varies according to:

1. **time** if $card\,(\{a_i,\ such\ as\ \exists\, a_i,\ a_j \in A,\ a_i(Val) \neq a_j(Val) \wedge a_i(Unit) = a_j(Unit) \wedge a_i(Date) \neq a_j(Date)\ \}) \geq k$
2. **place** if $card\,(\{a_i,\ such\ as\ \exists\, a_i,\ a_j \in A,\ a_i(Val) \neq a_j(Val) \wedge a_i(Unit) = a_j(Unit) \wedge a_i(Place) \neq a_j(Place)\ \}) \geq k$
3. **restriction** if $card\,(\{a_i,\ such\ as\ \exists\, a_i,\ a_j \in A,\ a_i(Val) \neq a_j(Val) \wedge a_i(Unit) = a_j(Unit) \wedge a_i(Restriction) \neq a_j(Restriction)\}) \geq k$
4. **time and place** if $(1) \wedge (2)$
5. **time and restriction** if $(1) \wedge (3)$
6. **place and restriction** if $(2) \wedge (3)$
7. **time, place and restriction** if $(1) \wedge (2) \wedge (3)$

Numerical values can be compared only if they have the same unit of measure. If not, they have to be converted.

For each criterion (time, place or restriction), only information of the same semantic type and of the same ontological level can be compared. For example, *metropolitan population* and *prison population* are restrictions of a different ontological level and cannot be compared. In the same way, place criteria can only be compared if they have the same ontological level: for example, prices *in Paris* and *in Toulouse* can be compared because the ontological level of both places is *city*. On the contrary, prices *in Paris* and *in France* cannot be compared since the ontological levels are respectively *city* and *country*. Several ontologies of geographical places exist, for example (Maurel and Piton, 1999) but a deep analysis of restrictions is necessary to identify the kind of implied knowledge.

In the particular cases where no information has been extracted for some criteria, it is also necessary to define some comparison rules. Thus, let $crit \in \{time,\ place,\ restriction\}$ and $a_i,\ a_j \in A$,
- if no information has been extracted for 2 compared criteria, then we consider that those criteria are equal (there is no information indicating that there is a variation according to those criteria), i.e. if $a_i(crit) = \emptyset$ and $a_j(crit) = \emptyset$, then

$a_i(crit) = a_j(crit)$
- if no information has been extracted for one of the 2 compared criteria, then we consider that those criteria are different (there is a variation), i.e. if $a_i(crit) = \emptyset$ and $a_j(crit) \neq \emptyset$, then $a_i(crit) \neq a_j(crit)$

In the example of figure 2, the price varies according to time, place and restriction. In the following example (figure 4), the price of gas varies according to time (*September 2005/* $\emptyset$) and place (*Paris/Toulouse*). For space reasons, we give only 2 frames for each example but it is obviously not sufficient to conclude.

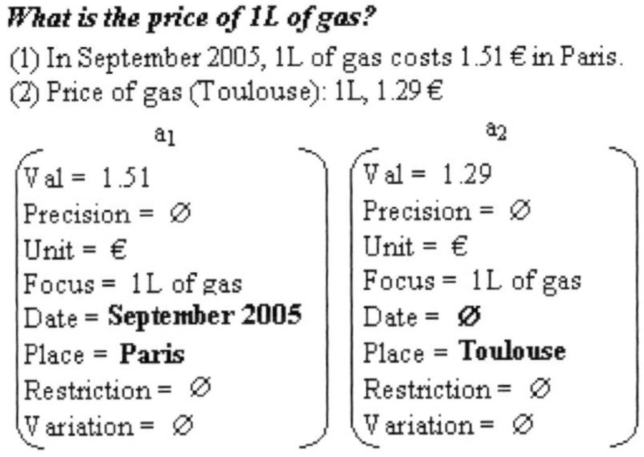

Figure 4: Example of variation

Variation criteria of numerical values are learnt from texts but can also be infered (or confirmed), for some domains, by common knowledge. For example, the triangle inequality states that for any three points x, y, z, we have:

distance(x, y) $\leq$ *distance(x, z)* $+$ *distance(z, y).*

From this, we can infer that a distance between two points vary according to restriction (itinerary).

In the following sections, we focus on numerical values which vary according to time.

3.3 Variation mode

The last step consists in identifying the variation mode of values. The idea is to draw a trend (increase, decrease, ...) of variaton in time so that an explanation can be generated. For this purpose, we have a set of couples (numerical value, date) representing the set of extracted answers. From this set, we draw a regression line (a line which comes as close to the points as possible) which determines the relationship between the two variables *value* and *date*.

The **correlation** between two variables reflects the degree to which the variables are related. In particular, Pearson's correlation (r) reflects the degree of linear relationship between two variables. It ranges from $+1$ to -1. A correlation of $+1$ means that there is a perfect positive linear relationship between variables. For example, figure 5 shows that a positive Pearson's correlation implies a general increase of values (trend) whereas a negative Pearson's correlation implies a general decrease. On the contrary, if r is low ($-0.6 < r < 0.6$), then the trend (increase or decrease) is mathematically considered as random[2].

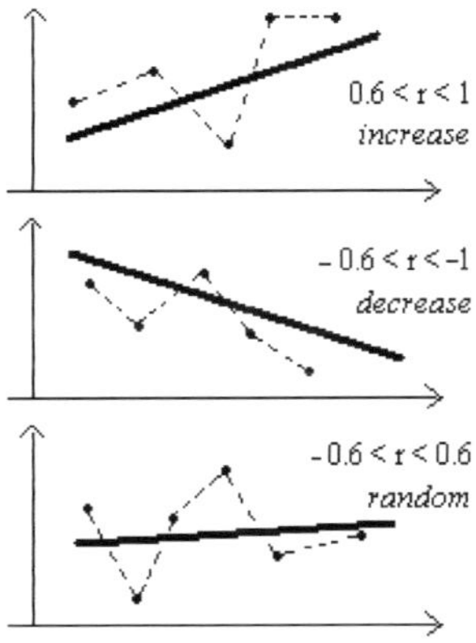

Figure 5: Variation mode

This method determines the variation mode of numerical values (it gives a variation trend) and determines if the values are strongly dependent on time or not (the highest r is, the more the numerical values are dependent on time).

Figure 6 shows the results for the question *How many inhabitants are there in France?* Different numerical values and associated dates are extracted from web pages. The Pearson's correlation is 0.682 meaning that the number of inhabitants increases according to time (between 1999 and 2005).

4 Answer generation

Once the searched numerical values have been extracted and characterized by their variation criteria and mode, a cooperative answer is generated in natural language. It is composed of two parts:

1. a direct answer if available,
2. an explanation of the value variation.

[2] Statistical Methods for Research Workers, R. Fisher (1925)

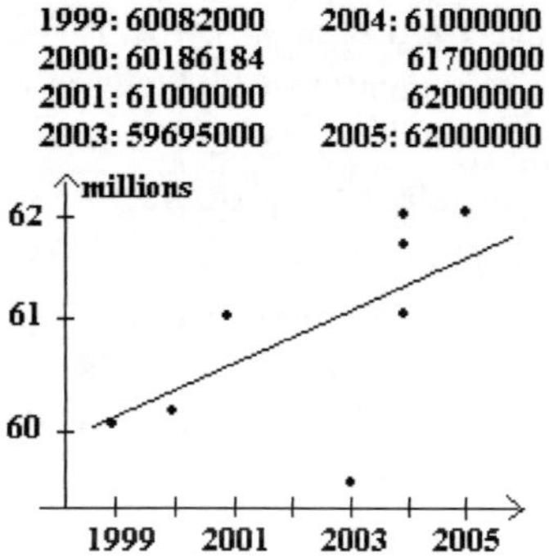

Figure 6: Variation mode: *How many inhabitants are there in France?*

In the following sections, we present some prerequisites to the construction of each of these parts in term of resources and knowledge.

4.1 Direct answer generation

There are mainly two cases: either one or several criteria are constrained by the question (as in *How many inhabitants are there in France in 2005?* where criteria of place and time are given), or some criteria are omitted (or implicit) (as in *How many inhabitants are there in France?* where there is no information on time). In the first case, the numerical value satisfying the constraints is chosen (unification between the criteria of the question and those extracted from web pages). In the second case, we assume that the user wants to have the most recent information.

We focus here on answers which vary according to time. Aberrant values are first filtered out by applying classical statistical methods. Then, when there is only one numerical value which satisfies the temporal constraint (given by the question or the most recent date), then the direct answer is generated from this value. When there is no numerical value satisfying the temporal constraint, only the second part of the answer (explanation) is generated.
In the case of several numerical values satisfying the temporal constraint, there may be approximate values. For example, the following answers (cf figure 6) are extracted for the question *How many inhabitants were there in France in 2004?*:
(1) *61.7 millions: number of inhabitants in France in 2004.*
(2) *In 2004, the French population is estimated to 61 millions.*
(3) *There are 62 millions of inhabitants in France in 2004.*

Each of these values is more or less approximate. The goal is then to identify which values are approximate and to decide which numerical value can be used for the generation task.

For that purpose, we proposed to 20 subjects a set of question-answer pairs. For each question, subjects were asked to choose one answer among a set of precise and approximate values and to explain why. For the previous question, 75% of the subjects prefer answer (1) because it is the most precise one, even if they consider it as an approximation. In majority, subjects explain that an approximate value is sufficient for great numbers and that values must not be rounded up (they proposed *61.7 millions* or *almost 62 millions* as an answer). On the contrary, subjects do not accept approximate values in the financial domain (price, salary, ...) but rather prefer an interval of values.

Thus, the direct answer is generated from the most precise numerical value if available. If all values are approximate, then the generated answer has to explain it: we plan to use prepositions of approximation (*about, almost, ...*) or linguistics clues which have been extracted from web pages (*precision* in the frames). The choice of a particular preposition depends on the degree of precision/approximation of numerical values: PrepNet (Saint-Dizier, 2005) provides a relatively deep description of preposition syntactic and semantic behaviours.

4.2 Explanation generation

Obviously, the generation of the cooperative part of the answer is the most complex because it requires complex lexical knowledge. We present briefly some of the necessary lexical resources. For example, verbs can be used in the answer to express numerical variations. Lexical descriptions are necessary and we use for that purpose a classification of French verbs (Saint-Dizier, 1999) based on the main classes defined by WordNet. The classes we are interested in for our task are mainly those of verbs of change (*increase, decrease*, etc.: in total, 262 verbs in French) and of verbs of movement (*climb, move forward/backward*, etc.: in total, 252 verbs in French) used metaphorically (Moriceau and Saint-Dizier, 2003). From these classes, we have characterized sub-classes of growth, decrease, etc., so that the lexicalisation task is constrained by the type of verbs which has to be used according to the variation mode (if verbs are extracted from web pages as linguistics clues of *variation*, they can also be reused in the answer).

A deep semantics of verbs (change, movement) is necessary to generate an answer which takes into account the characteristics of numerical variation as well as possible: for example, the variation mode but also the speed and range of the variation. Thus, for each sub-class of verbs and its associated variation mode, we need a refined description of ontological domains and selectional restrictions so that an appropriate verb lexicalisation can be chosen: which verb can be applied to prices, to age, etc.? We plan to use proportional series representing verb sub-classes according to the speed and amplitude of variation. For example, the use of *climb* (resp. *drop*) indicates a faster growth (resp. decrease) than *go up* (resp. *go down*): the verb *climb* is prefered for the generation of *The increase of gas prices climb to 20.3% in october 2005* whereas *go up* is prefered in *The increase of gas prices go up to 7.2% in september 2005*.
As for direct answer generation, verbs can possibly be associated with a preposition that refines the information (*The average age of marriage increased by* **about** *5.5 years between 1972 and 2005*).

5 Conclusion

In this paper, we presented an approach for the generation of cooperative numerical answers in a question-answering system. Our method allows us to generate:

(1) a correct synthetic answer over a whole set of data and,

(2) a cooperative part which explains the variation phenomenon to the user,

whenever several numerical values are extracted as possible answers to a question. Information is first extracted from web pages so that numerical values can be characterized: variation criteria and mode are then identified in order to generate explanation to the user. Several future directions are obviously considered:

- an analysis of needs for common knowledge so that the answer characterization task is made easier,
- an analysis of how restrictions are lexicalized in texts (adjectives, relative clauses, etc.) in order to extract them easily,
- an evaluation of the knowledge costs and of what domain specific is (especially for common knowledge about restrictions),
- an evaluation of the quality of answers proposed to users and of the utility of a user model for the selection of the best answer.

References

V. Dahl and H. Abramson. 1984. *On Gapping Grammars*. Proceedings of the Second Logic Programming Conference.

S. Harabagiu and F. Lacatusu. 2004. *Strategies for Advanced Question Answering*. Proceedings of the Workshop on Pragmatics of Question Answering at HLT-NAACL 2004.

D. Maurel and O. Piton. 1999. *Un dictionnaire de noms propres pour Intex: les noms propres géographiques*. Lingvisticae Investigationes, XXII, pp. 277-287, John Benjamins B. V., Amsterdam.

D.L. McGuinness and P. Pinheiro da Silva. 2004. *Trusting Answers on the Web*. New Directions in Question-Answering, chapter 22, Mark T. Maybury (ed), AAAI/MIT Press.

D. Moldovan, C. Clark, S. Harabagiu and S. Maiorano. 2003. *COGEX: A Logic Prover for Question Answering*. Proceedings of HLT-NAACL 2003.

V. Moriceau and P. Saint-Dizier. 2003. *A Conceptual Treatment of Metaphors for NLP*. Proceedings of ICON.

V. Moriceau. 2005. *Answer Generation with Temporal Data Integration*. Proceedings of ENLG'05.

D.R. Radev and K.R. McKeown. 1998. *Generating Natural Language Summaries from Multiple On-Line Sources*. Computational Linguistics, vol. 24, issue 3 - Natural Language Generation, pp. 469 - 500.

P. Saint-Dizier. 1999. *Alternations and Verb Semantic Classes for French*. Predicative Forms for NL and LKB, Kluwer Academic.

P. Saint-Dizier. 2005. *PrepNet: a Framework for Describing Prepositions: preliminary investigation results*. Proccedings of IWCS'05.

B. Webber, C. Gardent and J. Bos. 2002. *Position statement: Inference in Question Answering*. Proceedings of LREC.

Incorporating User Models in Question Answering to Improve Readability

Silvia Quarteroni and **Suresh Manandhar**
Department of Computer Science
University of York
York YO10 5DD
United Kingdom
{silvia,suresh}@cs.york.ac.uk

Abstract

Most question answering and information retrieval systems are insensitive to different users' needs and preferences, as well as their reading level. In (Quarteroni and Manandhar, 2006), we introduce a hybrid QA-IR system based on a a user model.
In this paper we focus on how the system filters and re-ranks the search engine results for a query according to their reading difficulty, providing user-tailored answers.
Keywords: *question answering, information retrieval, user modelling, readability.*

1 Introduction

Question answering (QA) systems are information retrieval systems accepting queries in natural language and returning the results in the form of sentences (or paragraphs, or phrases). They move beyond standard information retrieval (IR) where results are presented in the form of a ranked list of query-relevant documents. Such a finer answer presentation is possible thanks to the application of computational linguistics techniques in order to filter irrelevant documents, and of a consistent amount of question pre-processing and result post-processing.

However, in most state-of-the-art QA systems the output remains independent of the questioner's characteristics, goals and needs; in other words, there is a lack of *user modelling*. For instance, an elementary school child and a University history student would get the same answer to the question: "*When did the Middle Ages begin?*".

Secondly, most QA systems focus on *factoid* questions, i.e. questions concerning people, dates, numerical quantities etc., which can generally be answered by a short sentence or phrase (Kwok et al., 2001). The mainstream approach to QA evaluation, represented by TREC-QA campaigns[1], has long fostered the criterion that a "good" system is one that returns the "correct" answer in the shortest possible formulation. Although recent efforts in TREC 2003 and 2004 (Voorhees, 2003; Voorhees, 2004) denoted an interest towards list questions and definitional (or "other") questions, we believe that there has not been enough interest towards non-factoid *answers*. The real issue is "realizing" that the answer to a question is sometimes too complex to be formulated and evaluated as a factoid: some queries have multiple, complex or controversial answers (take e.g. "*What were the causes of World War II?*"). In such situations, returning a short paragraph or text snippet is more appropriate than exact answer spotting. For instance, the answer to "*What is a metaphor?*" may be better understood with the inclusion of examples. This viewpoint is supported by recent user behaviour studies which showed that even in the case of factoid-based QA systems, the most eligible result format consisted in a paragraph where the sentence containing the answer was highlighted (Lin et al., 2003).

The issue of non-factoids is related to the user modelling problem: while factoid answers do not necessarily require to be contextualized within the user's knowledge and viewpoint, the need is much stronger in the case of definitions, explanations and descriptions. This is mentioned in the TREC 2003 report (Voorhees, 2003) when discussing the evaluation of definitional questions: however, the issue is expeditiously solved by assuming a fixed user profile (the "average news reader").

We are currently developing an *adaptive* system which adjusts its output with respect to a user model. The system can be seen as an enhanced IR system which adapts both the content and presentation of the final results, improving their *quality*.

[1] http://trec.nist.gov

In this paper, we show that QA systems can benefit from the contribution of user models, and explain how these can be used to filter the information presented as an answer based on readability. Eventually, we describe preliminary results obtained via an evaluation framework inspired by user-centered search engine evaluation.

2 System Architecture

The high-level architecture as represented in Figure 1 shows the basic components of the system, the QA module and the user model.

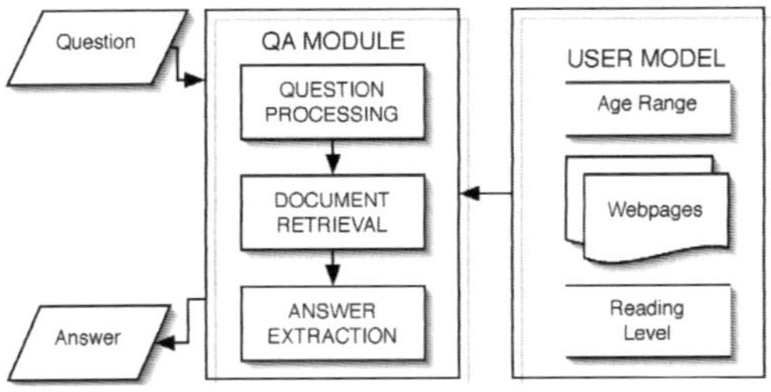

Figure 1: High level system architecture

The QA module, described in the following section, is organized according to the three-tier partition underlying most state-of-the-art systems: 1) question processing, 2) document retrieval, 3) answer generation. The module makes use of a web search engine for document retrieval and consults the user model to obtain the criteria to filter and re-rank the search engine results and to eventually present them appropriately to the user.

2.1 User model

Depending on the application of interest, the user model (UM) can be designed to suit the information needs of the QA module in different ways. Our current application, YourQA[2], is a learning-oriented system to help students find information on the Web for their assignments. Our UM consists of the user's:

- age range, $a \in \{7-11, 11-16, adult\}$
- reading level, $r \in \{poor, medium, good\}$
- webpages of interest/bookmarks, w

The age range parameter has been chosen to match the partition between primary school, contemporary school and higher education age in Britain; our reading level parameter takes three values which ideally (but not necessarily) correspond to the three age ranges and may be further refined in the future for more fine-grained modelling.

Analogies can be found with the SeAn (Ardissono et al., 2001), and SiteIF (Magnini and Strapparava, 2001) news recommender systems, where information such as age and browsing history, resp. are part of the UM. More generally, our approach is similar to that of personalized search systems (Teevan et al., 2005; Pitkow et al., 2002), which construct UMs based on the user's documents and webpages.

In our system, UM information is explicitly collected from the user; while age and reading level are self-assessed, the user's interests are extracted from the document set w using a keyphrase extractor (see further for details). Eventually, a dialogue framework with a history component will contribute to the construction and update of the user model in a less intruding and thus more user-friendly way. In this paper we focus on how to adapt search result presentation using the reading level parameter: age and webpages will not be discussed.

2.2 Related work

Non-factoids and user modelling As mentioned above, the TREC-QA evaluation campaign, to which the vast majority of current QA systems abide, mainly approaches factoid-based answers. To our knowledge, our system is among the first to address the need for a different approach to non-factoid *answers*. The structure of our QA component reflects the typical structure of a web-based QA system in its three-tier composition. Analogies in this can be found for instance in MULDER (Kwok et al., 2001), which is organized according to a question processing/answer extraction/passage ranking pipeline. However, a significant aspect of novelty in our architecture is that the QA component is supported by the user model.

Additionally, we have changed the relative importance of the different tiers: while we drastically reduce linguistic processing during question processing and answer generation, we give more relief to the post-retrieval phase and to the role of the UM. Having removed the need for fine-grained answer spotting, the emphasis is shifted towards finding closely connected sentences that are highly

[2] `http://www.cs.york.ac.uk/aig/aqua`

relevant to answer the query.

Readability Within computational linguistics, several applications have been designed to address the needs of users with low reading skills. The computational approach to textual adaptation is commonly based on *natural language generation*: the process "translate" a difficult text into a syntactically and lexically simpler version. In the case of PSET (Carroll et al., 1999) for instance, a tagger, a morphological analyzer and generator and a parser are used to reformulate newspaper text for users affected by aphasia. Another interesting research is Inui et al.'s lexical and syntactical paraphrasing system for deaf students (Inui et al., 2003). In this system, the judgment of experts (teachers) is used to learn selection rules for paraphrases acquired using various methods (statistical, manual, etc.). In the SKILLSUM project (Williams and Reiter, 2005), used to generate literacy test reports, a set of choices regarding output (cue phrases, ordering and punctuation) are taken by a micro-planner based on a set of rules.

Our approach is conceptually different from the above: exploiting the wealth of information available in the context of a Web-based QA system, we can afford to *choose* among the documents available on a given subject those which best suit our readability requirements. This is possible thanks to the versatility of language modelling, which allows us to tailor the readability estimation of documents to any kind of user profile in a dynamic manner, as explained in section 3.2.3.

3 QA Module

In this section we discuss the information flow among the subcomponents of the QA module (see Figure 2 for a representative diagram) and focus on reading level estimation and document filtering. For further details on the implementation of the QA module, see (Quarteroni and Manandhar, 2006).

3.1 Question Processing

The first step performed by YourQA is query expansion: additional queries are created replacing question terms with synonyms using WordNet[3].

[3]http://wordnet.princeton.edu

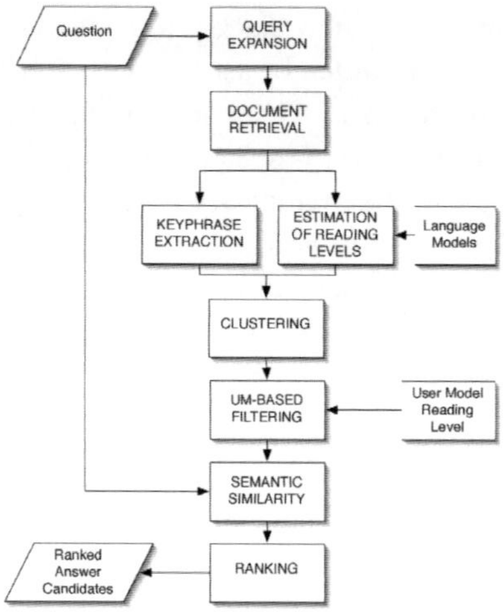

Figure 2: Diagram of the QA module

3.2 Retrieval and Result Processing

3.2.1 Document retrieval

We use Google[4] to retrieve the top 20 documents returned for each of the queries issued from the query expansion phase. The subsequent steps will progressively narrow the parts of these documents where relevant information is located.

3.2.2 Keyphrase extraction

Keyphrase extraction is useful in two ways: first, it produces features to group the retrieved documents thematically during the clustering phase, and thus enables to present results by groups. Secondly, when the document parameter (w) of the UM is active, matches are sought between the keyphrases extracted from the documents and those extracted from the user's set of interesting documents; thus it is possible to prioritize results which are more compatible with his/her interests.

Hence, once the documents are retrieved, we extract their keyphrases using Kea (Witten et al., 1999), an extractor based on Naïve Bayes classification. Kea first splits each document into phrases and then takes short subsequences of these initial phrases as candidate keyphrases. Two attributes are used to classify a phrase p as a keyphrase or a non-keyphrase: its TF $\times$ IDF score within the set of retrieved documents and the index of p's first appearance in the document. Kea outputs a ranked list of phrases, among which we select the top three as keyphrases for each of our documents.

[4]http://www.google.com

3.2.3 Estimation of reading levels

In order to adjust search result presentation to the user's reading ability, we estimate the reading difficulty of each retrieved document using the Smoothed Unigram Model, a variation of a Multinomial Bayes classifier (Collins-Thompson and Callan, 2004). Whereas other popular approaches such as Flesch-Kincaid (Kincaid et al., 1975) are based on sentence length, the language modelling approach accounts especially for lexical information. The latter has been found to be more effective as the former when approaching the reading level of subjects in primary and secondary school age (Collins-Thompson and Callan, 2004). Moreover, it is more applicable than length-based approach for Web documents, where sentences are typically short regardless of the complexity of the text.

The language modelling approach proceeds in two phases: in the training phase, given a range of reading levels, a set of representative documents is collected for each reading level. A unigram language model lm_s is then built for each set s; the model consists of a list of the word stems appearing in the training documents with their individual probabilities. Textual readability is not modelled at a conceptual level: thus complex concepts explained in simple words might be classified as suitable even for a poor reading level; However we have observed that in most Web documents lexical, syntactic and conceptual complexity are usually consistent within documents, hence it makes sense to apply a reasoning-free technique without impairing readability estimation. Our unigram language models account for the following reading levels:
1) *poor*, i.e. suitable for ages 7 – 11;
2) *medium*, suitable for ages 11–16;
3) *good*, suitable for adults.
This partition in three groups has been chosen to suit the training data available for our school application, which consists of about 180 HTML pages (mostly from the "BBC schools"[5], "Think Energy"[6], "Cassini Huygens resource for schools"[7] and "Magic Keys storybooks"[8] websites), explicitly annotated by the publishers according to the reading levels above.

In the test phase, given an unclassified document D, the estimated reading level of D is the language model lm_i maximizing the likelihood $L(lm_i|D)$ that D has been generated by lm_i. Such likelihood is estimated using the formula:

$$L(lm_i|D) = \sum_{w \in D} C(w, D) \cdot log(P(w|lm_i))$$

where w is a word in the document, $C(w, d)$ represents the number of occurrences of w in D and $P(w|lm_i)$ is the probability that w occurs in lm_i (approached by its frequency).

An advantage of language modelling is its portability, since it is quite quick to create word stem/frequency histograms on the fly. This implies that models can be produced to represent more fine-grained reading levels as well as the specific requirements of a single user: the only necessary information are sets of training documents representing each level to be modelled.

3.2.4 Clustering

As an indicator of inter-document relatedness, we use document clustering (Steinbach et al., 2000) to group them using both their estimated reading difficulty and their topic (i.e. their keyphrases). In particular we use a hierarchical algorithm, Cobweb (implemented using the WEKA suite of tools (Witten and Frank, 2000) as it produces a cluster tree which is visually simple to analyse: each leaf corresponds to one document, and sibling leaves denote documents that are strongly related both in topic and in reading difficulty. Figure 3 illustrates an example cluster tree for the the query: *"Who painted the Sistine chapel?"*. Leaf labels represent document keyphrases extracted by Kea for the corresponding documents and ovals represent non-terminal nodes in the cluster tree (these are labelled using the most common keyphrases in their underlying leaves).

3.3 Answer Extraction

The purpose of answer extraction is to present the most interesting excerpts of the retrieved documents according to both the user's query topics and reading level. This process, presented in sections 3.3.1 – 3.3.4, follows the diagram in Figure 2: we use the UM to filter the clustered documents, then compute the similarity between the question and the filtered document passages in order to return the best ones in a ranked list.

[5]`http://bbc.co.uk/schools`
[6]`http://www.think-energy.com`
[7]`http://www.pparc.ac.uk/Ed/ch/Home.htm`
[8]`http://www.magickeys.com/books/`

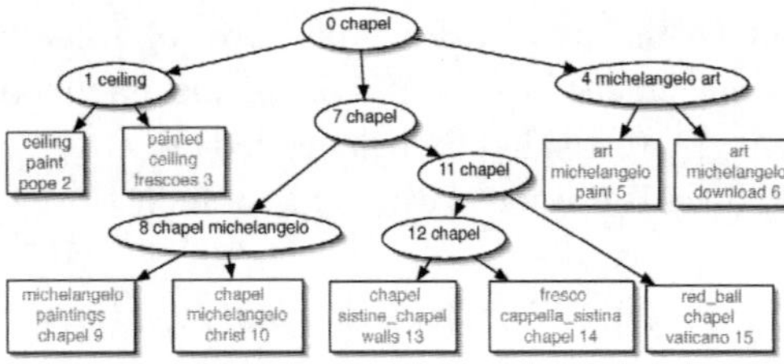

Figure 3: Cluster tree for *"Who painted the Sistine chapel?"*. Leaf 3 and the leaves grouped under nodes 8 and 12 represent documents with an estimated good reading level; leaf 15 and the leaves underlying node 4 have a medium reading level; leaf 2 represents a poor reading level document.

3.3.1 UM-based filtering

The documents in the cluster tree are filtered according to the UM reading level, r: only those compatible with the user's reading ability are retained for further analysis. However, if the number of retained documents does not exceed a given threshold, we accept in our candidate set part of the documents having the next lowest readability in case $r \in \{good, medium\}$ or a medium readability in case $r = poor$.

3.3.2 Semantic similarity

Within each of the documents retained, we seek for the sentences which are semantically most relevant to the query. Given a sentence p and the query q, we represent them as two sets of words $\mathcal{P} = \{pw_1, \ldots, pw_m\}$ and $\mathcal{Q} = \{qw_1, \ldots, qw_n\}$. The semantic distance from p to q is then:
$dist_q(p) = \sum_{1 \leq i \leq m} min_j[d(pw_i, qw_j)]$
where $d(pw_i, qw_j)$ represents the Jiang-Conrath word-level distance between pw_i and qw_j (Jiang and Conrath, 1997), based on WordNet 2.0. The intuition is that for each question word, we find the word in the candidate answer sentence which minimizes the word-level distance and then we compute the sum of such minima.

3.3.3 Passage and cluster ranking

For a given document, we can thus isolate a sentence s minimizing the distance to the query. The passage P, i.e. a window of up to 5 sentences centered on s, will be a candidate result. We assign to such passage a *score* equal to the similarity of s to the query; in turn, the score of P is used as the score of the document containing it. We also define a ranking function for clusters, which allows to order them according to the maximal score of their component documents. Passages from the highest ranking cluster will be presented first to the user, in decreasing order of score, followed by the passages from lower ranking clusters.

3.3.4 Answer presentation

To present our answers, we fix a threshold for the number of results to be returned following the ranking exposed above. Each result consists of a title and document passage where the sentence which best answers the query is highlighted; the URL of the original document is also available for loading if the user finds the passage interesting and wants to read more.

4 Results

We report the results of running our system on a range of queries, which include factoid/simple, complex and controversial questions[9].

4.1 Simple answer

As an example of a simple query, we present the results for: *"Who painted the Sistine Chapel?"*, the system returned the following passages:
—UM_{good}: ***"Sistine Chapel (sis-teen). A chapel adjoining Saint Peter's Basilica, noted for the frescoes of biblical subject painted by Michelangelo on its walls and ceilings."***
—UM_{med}: ***"In all Michelangelo painted more than 300 different figures on the Sistine Chapel ceiling."***
—UM_{poor}: ***"My name is Jacopo L'Indaco and I was an assistant to Michelangelo when he painted the Sistine Chapel."***
To obtain the above answers the system was run 3 times with different values for the reading level parameter in the UM, as defined in 3.2.3. As we can see, in all cases the correct information is present although not always explicitly, as in the first two cases. This is because our current semantic similarity metric only operates at word level. In this example, all sentences containing "painted", "Sistine" and "Chapel" obtain a distance of 0 to the query, regardless of their formulation. Also notice how the difference in language complexity is clearly discernible in the different answers.

4.2 Complex answer

We illustrate the results of our system with the query *"Definition of metaphor"*, which relates to a difficult concept. Our top results, highlighted in

[9]Notice that this partition is not to be interpreted as a methodological division, as we currently approach complex and controversial answers the same way.

boldface within their containing passages, are:

—UM_{good}: *"**Definition of Metaphor. Metaphor is a process by which we conceive "one thing in terms of another, and its primary function is understanding" (Lakoff and Johnson, Metaphors We Live By 36).** That is, we often do (and must) talk about things that do not physically exist, that we cannot reach out and touch or take apart with our hands to see what is inside and how it works: love, time, anger, life. [...] We make them tangible by, in a process of thought, applying models of physical things to them: love is falling; argument is war. "*

—UM_{med}: *"**Definition: A metaphor is a figure of speech that compares unlike things by saying that one thing is the other.** Often metaphors are simple comparisons, but they can be extended so that different aspects of the things compared are treated separately. "*

—UM_{poor}: *we did not find any document exactly matching the reading level, we thus returned the results for UM_{med} (see above).*

As before, there is a clear difference in the language complexity of the two answers.

4.3 Controversial answer

We illustrate this case using the query *"Who wrote the Iliad?"*, which is a subject of debate: the existence of a single author, as well as the historicity of the poet Homer are under discussion. These are among our top results:

—UM_{good}: *"Most Classicists would agree that, whether there was ever such a composer as "Homer" or not, the Homeric poems are the product of an oral tradition, a generations-old technique that was the collective inheritance of many singer-poets, aoidoi. [...] **Could the Iliad and Odyssey have been oral-formulaic poems, composed on the spot by the poet using a collection of memorized traditional verses and phases?"***

—UM_{med}: *"No reliable ancient evidence for Homer – earliest traditions involve conjecture (e.g. conflicting claims to be his place of origin) and legend (e.g. Homer as son of river-god). **General ancient assumption that same poet wrote Iliad and Odyssey (and possibly other poems) questioned by many modern scholars: differences explained biographically in ancient world (e g wrote Od. in old age); but similarities could be due to imitation."***

—UM_{poor}: ***"Homer wrote The Iliad and The Odyssey (at least, supposedly a blind bard named "Homer" did)."***

In this case we can see how the problem of attribution of the *Iliad* is made clearly visible: in the three results, document passages provide a context which helps to explain such controversy at different levels of difficulty.

5 Evaluation

5.1 Methodology

Our system is not a QA system in the strict sense, as it does not single out one correct answer phrase. The key objective is an improved satisfaction of the user towards its adaptive results, which are hopefully more suitable to his reading level. A user-centred evaluation methodology that assesses how the system meets individual information needs is therefore more appropriate for YourQA than TREC-QA metrics.

We draw our evaluation guidelines from (Su, 2003), which proposes a comprehensive search engine evaluation model. We define the following metrics (see Table 1):

1. *Relevance*:
   - strict precision (P_1): the ratio between the number of results rated as relevant and all the returned results,
   - loose precision (P_2): the ratio between the number of results rated as relevant or partially relevant and all the returned results.
2. *User satisfaction*: a 7-point Likert scale[10] is used to assess satisfaction with:
   - loose precision of results (S_1),
   - query success (S_2).
3. *Reading level accuracy (A_r)*. This metric was not present in (Su, 2003) and has been introduced to assess the reading level estimation. Given the set $\mathcal{R}$ of results returned by the system for a reading level r, it is the ratio between the number of documents $\in \mathcal{R}$ rated by the users as suitable for r and $|\mathcal{R}|$. We compute A_r for each reading level.
4. *Overall utility (U)*: the search session as a whole is assessed via a 7-point Likert scale.

We have discarded some of the metrics proposed by (Su, 2003) when they appeared as linked to technical aspects of search engines (e.g. connectivity), and when response time was concerned as at the present stage this has not been considered

[10] This measure – ranging from 1= "extremely unsatisfactory" to 7="extremely satisfactory" – is particularly suitable to assess the degree to which the system meets the user's search needs. It was reported in (Su, 1991) as the best single measure for information retrieval among 20 tested.

an issue. Also, we exclude metrics relating to the user interface which are not relevant for this study.

Metric	*field*	*description*
Relevance	P_1	strict precision
	P_2	loose precision
Satisfaction	S_1	with loose precision
	S_2	with query success
Accuracy	A_g	good reading level
	A_m	medium reading level
	A_p	poor reading level
Utility	U	overall session

Table 1: Summary of evaluation metrics

5.2 Evaluation results

We performed our evaluation by running 24 queries (partly reported in Table 3) on both Google and YourQA[11]. The results – i.e. snippets from the Google result page and passages returned by YourQA – were given to 20 evaluators. These were aged between 16 and 52, all having a self-assessed good or medium English reading level. They came from various backgrounds (University students/graduates, professionals, high school) and mother-tongues. Evaluators filled in a questionnaire assessing the relevance of each passage, the success and result readability of the single queries, and the overall utility of the system; values were thus computed for the metrics in Table 1.

	P_1	P_2	S_1	S_2	U
Google	0,39	0,63	4,70	4,61	4,59
YourQA	0,51	0,79	5,39	5,39	5,57

Table 2: Evaluation results

5.2.1 Relevance

The precision results (see Table 2) for the whole search session were computed by averaging the values obtained for the 20 queries. Although quite close, they show a 10-15% difference in favour of the YourQA system for both strict precision (P_1) and loose precision (P_2). This suggests that the coarse semantic processing applied and the visualisation of the context contribute to the creation of more relevant passages.

[11]To make the two systems more comparable, we turned off query expansion and only submitted the original question sentence

5.2.2 User satisfaction

After each query, we asked evaluators the following questions: *"How would you rate the ratio of relevant/partly relevant results returned?"* (assessing S_1) and *"How would you rate the success of this search?"* (assessing S_2). Table 2 denotes a higher level of satisfaction tributed to the YourQA system in both cases.

5.2.3 Reading level accuracy

Adaptivity to the users' reading level is the distinguishing feature of the YourQA system: we were thus particularly interested in its performance in this respect. Table 3 shows that altogether, evaluators found our results appropriate for the reading levels to which they were assigned. The accuracy tended to decrease (from 94% to 72%) with the level: this was predictable as it is more constraining to conform to a lower reading level than to a higher one. However this also suggests that our estimation of document difficulty was perhaps too "optimisitic": we are currently working with better quality training data which allows to obtain more accurate language models.

Query	A_g	A_m	A_p
Who painted the Sistine Chapel?	0,85	0,72	0,79
Who was the first American in space?	0,94	0,80	0,72
Who was Achilles' best friend?	1,00	0,98	0,79
When did the Romans invade Britain?	0,87	0,74	0,82
Definition of metaphor	0,95	0,81	0,38
What is chickenpox?	1,00	0,97	0,68
Define german measles	1,00	0,87	0,80
Types of rhyme	1,00	1,00	0,79
Who was a famous cubist?	0,90	0,75	0,85
When did the Middle Ages begin?	0,91	0,82	0,68
Was there a Trojan war?	0,97	1,00	0,83
Shakespeare's most famous play?	0,90	0,97	0,83
average	**0,94**	**0,85**	**0,72**

Table 3: Queries and reading level accuracy

5.2.4 Overall utility

At the end of the whole search session, users answered the question: *"Overall, how was this search session?"* relating to their search experience with Google and the YourQA system. The values obtained for U in Table 2 show a clear preference (a difference of $\simeq 1$ on the 7-point scale) of the users for YourQA, which is very positive considering that it represents their general judgement on the system.

5.3 Future work

We plan to run a larger evaluation by including more metrics, such as user *vs* system ranking of results and the contribution of cluster by cluster presentation. We intend to conduct an evaluation also involving users with a poor reading level, so that each evaluator will only examine answers targeted to his/her reading level. We will analyse our results with respect to the individual reading levels and the different types of questions proposed.

6 Conclusion

A user-tailored open domain QA system is outlined where a user model contributes to elaborating answers corresponding to the user's needs and presenting them efficiently. In this paper we have focused on how the user's reading level (a parameter in the UM) can be used to filter and re-order the candidate answer passages. Our preliminary results show a positive feedback from human assessors on the utility of the system in an information seeking domain. Our short term goals involve performing a more extensive evaluation, exploiting more UM parameters in answer selection and implementing a dialogue interface to improve the system's interactivity.

References

L. Ardissono, L. Console, and I. Torre. 2001. An adaptive system for the personalized access to news. *AI Commun.*, 14(3):129–147.

J. Carroll, G. Minnen, D. Pearce, Y. Canning, S. Devlin, and J. Tait. 1999. Simplifying text for language-impaired readers. In *Proceedings of EACL'99*, pages 269–270.

K. Collins-Thompson and J. P. Callan. 2004. A language modeling approach to predicting reading difficulty. In *Proceedings of HLT/NAACL*.

K. Inui, A. Fujita, T. Takahashi, R. Iida, and T. Iwakura. 2003. Text simplification for reading assistance: a project note. In *ACL Workshop on Paraphrasing: Paraphrase Acquisition and Applications*, pages 9–16.

J. J. Jiang and D. W. Conrath. 1997. Semantic similarity based on corpus statistics and lexical taxonomy. In *Proceedings of the International Conference Research on Computational Linguistics (ROCLING X)*.

J. Kincaid, R. Fishburne, R. Rodgers, and B. Chissom. 1975. Derivation of new readability formulas for navy enlisted personnel. Technical Report Branch Report 8-75, Chief of Naval Training.

C. C. T. Kwok, O. Etzioni, and D. S. Weld. 2001. Scaling question answering to the web. In *World Wide Web*, pages 150–161.

J. Lin, D. Quan, V. Sinha, and K Bakshi. 2003. What makes a good answer? the role of context in question answering. In *Proceedings of INTERACT 2003*.

Bernardo Magnini and Carlo Strapparava. 2001. Improving user modelling with content-based techniques. In *UM: Proceedings of the 8th Int. Conference*, volume 2109 of *LNCS*. Springer.

James Pitkow, Hinrich Schuetze, Todd Cass, Rob Cooley, Don Turnbull, Andy Edmonds, Eytan Adar, and Thomas Breuel. 2002. Personalized search. *Commun. ACM*, 45(9):50–55.

S. Quarteroni and S. Manandhar. 2006. User modelling for adaptive question answering and information retrieval. In *Proceedings of FLAIRS'06*.

M. Steinbach, G. Karypid, and V. Kumar. 2000. A comparison of document clustering techniques.

L. T. Su. 1991. *An investigation to find appropriate measures for evaluating interactive information retrieval*. Ph.D. thesis, New Brunswick, NJ, USA.

L. T. Su. 2003. A comprehensive and systematic model of user evaluation of web search engines: Ii. an evaluation by undergraduates. *J. Am. Soc. Inf. Sci. Technol.*, 54(13):1193–1223.

Jaime Teevan, Susan T. Dumais, and Eric Horvitz. 2005. Personalizing search via automated analysis of interests and activities. In *Proceedings of SIGIR '05*, pages 449–456, New York, NY, USA. ACM Press.

E. M. Voorhees. 2003. Overview of the TREC 2003 question answering track. In *Text REtrieval Conference*.

E. M. Voorhees. 2004. Overview of the TREC 2004 question answering track. In *Text REtrieval Conference*.

S. Williams and E. Reiter. 2005. Generating readable texts for readers with low basic skills. In *Proceedings of ENLG-2005*, pages 140–147.

H. Witten and E. Frank. 2000. *Data Mining: Practical Machine Learning Tools and Techniques with Java Implementation*. Morgan Kaufmann.

I. H. Witten, G. W. Paynter, E. Frank, C. Gutwin, and C. G. Nevill-Manning. 1999. KEA: Practical automatic keyphrase extraction. In *ACM DL*, pages 254–255.

Association for Computational Linguistics
209 N. Eighth Street
Stroudsburg, Pennsylvania 18360

Interactive Question Answering Workshop 2006

Held at HLT/NAACL 2006

New York, New York, USA
8-9 June 2006

ISBN: 978-1-61738-491-2